PRESERVING THE PERSON

A Look at the Human Sciences

C. STEPHEN EVANS

BAKER BOOK HOUSE

Grand Rapids, Michigan 49506

To Kelley Elaine

in the hope that she will
be a whole person

ISBN: 0-8010-3385-3
Library of Congress Catalog
Card Number: 77-26551

Printed in the United
States of America

1 **The Problem: The Attack on the Person**   9
What Is a Person?   10
Justice and the Personal   11
The Demise of the Person   14
What Makes Science Scientific?   15
The Prestige of Science   18
Summary and Preview   19

2 **Minds and Brains: The Person as Machine**   21
Descartes and the World Knot   21
Three Challenges to Dualism   23
The Brain: A Thinking Machine   29
Unanswered Questions   31

3 **The Loss of the Person in Psychology: Freud**   35
Freud and Psychoanalysis   35
The Biological Basis of Mind   36
Freud's Critics Respond   40
Presuppositions: The Real Difference   42

4 **The Loss of the Person in Psychology: Behaviorism**   45
Behaviorism as Science: Watson and Skinner   45
Inner Mental States   48
Operant Conditioning   52
A Question of Control   53
Survival: The Final Value   55

5 **The Loss of the Person in Sociology**   59
Sociology as Science: Durkheim   60
Functionalism   62
Ideology   64
The Question of Values   66

6 **Feeling the Loss: Why Care?**   69
Agents, Events and Acts   70
Epistemology and the Loss of the Personal   74
Morality and the Loss of the Personal   79
Political Theory and the Loss of the Personal   82

7 **Grappling with the Loss** 87
Contradiction or Resolution? 87
Six Routes to Resolution 88
Ideal Types 91

8 **Reinterpreters of the Personal** 93
Capitulators 95
Compatibilists 97

9 **Limiters of Science** 101
Territorialists 102
Perspectivalists 105
Two Perspectivalists: Jeeves and MacKay 108

10 **Humanizers of Science** 119
The Hypothetico-Deductive Method 119
Particularists 122
Generalists 132
Difficulties of Humanizing Science 136

11 **Recovering the Person: Thinking Christianly about Man** 139
Christianity and Culture 139
In the Image of God 142
Biblical Dualism or Biblical Monism 148
Of Poems and Persons 149
A Model for Integration 152

12 **Man in a Personal Universe** 159
The Tenacity of Reductionism 160
The Contribution of Christian Theism 162
Agents and Observers 165
The Reality of the Personal 168
Notes 170
Index 176

preface

The human quest for self-understanding is ancient. The attempt to "know thyself" transcends the parochial boundaries between such academic disciplines as psychology, sociology, philosophy and theology. The reason for this is that this quest is not essentially academic; it is a human quest, pursued by persons in every age. It is in this spirit that a philosopher by vocation and a Christian by conviction dares to reflect on what he terms the human sciences to assess their contribution to this self-understanding.

That contribution is great. But it has raised many profound questions for those asking, "Who am I?" Is the image of human personhood which emerges from these sciences compatible with the understanding which dominated Western thought for centuries: the traditional vision of the person as a free soul who at least partially transcends his environment? Or must that "traditional" vision be abandoned as unscientific? What has happened to the traditional questions asked by "psychologists" in their pre-twentieth-century unscientific days? Is man free? Does he possess a soul? What is the nature of soul? And, of course, these questions involve others, chiefly those concerning moral responsibility and life after death, questions which still grip twentieth-century persons. It goes without saying that these questions are peculiarly important to a Christian who believes in moral responsibility and the life everlasting. What does it mean in the twentieth century to believe that man, male and female, was created in the image of God?

These are the questions which this essay ultimately addresses. It does so in a spirit of tentativeness, hopeful of stimulating further thought on the part of reflective people, modestly recognizing that any work of this sort is a progress report, subject to correction and revision.

I should like to thank the students of Wheaton College, particularly those in Philosophy 51, for serving as sounding boards and critics for these ideas, and for stimulating many of them with their fierce questioning and intense concern for the issues. I wish to extend a special word of appreciation to the Aldeen Fund which provided support enabling me to bring this book to completion. The list of others to whom I am indebted is long. Arthur Holmes, who has done more to inspire and shape my philosophical thought than any other human being, read the manuscript at an early stage. Ron Burwell of King's College, Don Postema of Bethel College, Nicholas Wolterstorff of Calvin College and Mark Cosgrove of Taylor University all read the manuscript, and it has benefited greatly from their criticisms. Cindy Koechling spent many long hours away from her family deciphering my handwriting to produce a readable manuscript. My wife Jan, who is a constant encouragement, had more to do with making this book a reality than she could know or I could say. To all of these splendid people, "persons" in the fullest sense, I say a heartfelt "thank you."

the problem: the attack on the person

Despite an unending stream of books designed to show that Christianity and science do not conflict, the viability of the Christian faith in a scientific culture remains a live issue. When someone reads about the "conflict" of science and religion, he is likely to encounter the famous attempt by the church to suppress the views of Galileo. Or perhaps the issue of evolution comes to mind, a controversy forever to be associated with the famous Scopes trial. These controversies are by now familiar, and if the latter does not yet seem as unnecessary, misguided, and rooted in misunderstanding as the former, it at least seems to lack the burning urgency and acrimony it had fifty years ago.

But many people, including many religious believers, seem to be unaware that an intellectual battle is currently raging—a battle whose implications for the Christian faith are so enormous that those earlier controversies almost seem incidental and peripheral. In fact, the importance of the earlier battle concerning evolution may be that it served as a preliminary skirmish to the current controversy. This current battle is the latest engagement in a very long war—the struggle over the nature of man. It is a battle which has been precipitated by the rise of new and powerful sciences dealing with man: physiology (particularly of the brain), psychology, sociology and that whole cluster of disciplines variously referred to as the behavioral sciences or sometimes the social sciences. What is at stake in this battle is the very notion of personhood. Are human beings *persons* in the sense in which that word has been traditionally understood?

what is a person?

What is a person? That question cannot be adequately answered in a few pages. Nevertheless in ordinary life the term is used with at least some measure of understanding, and it is possible to single out some of the concepts that are crucial to the notion of personhood.

Persons are first of all *agents*. They are beings who make *choices* and then act on those decisions. Persons are also *conscious*. Though they sometimes act blindly or unconsciously, they possess a degree of intellectual awareness, including that special type of reflective awareness usually referred to as *self-consciousness*.

Persons are hardly to be thought of as mere (purely rational) thinking machines, however, for they are not always rational in their behavior. In fact their acts seem to stem more from what they *value* than from what they know. Persons desire, love, want, wish, dislike, abhor and generally adopt a multitude of caring attitudes towards a complex variety of things.

Persons, moreover, act for certain *purposes* and goals, and they often defend their acts by citing *reasons* of various sorts. Persons think of at least some of their decisions and acts as *free,* and they are held to be *responsible* for those acts. As responsible agents, persons are usually regarded as unique individuals with a measure of autonomy. But this individuality hardly precludes their involvement in larger groups. In fact, to understand a person's individuality, we usually think of him in terms of the *communities* of which he is a part, and which certainly are in some sense part of him.

Despite all this complexity, persons are nonetheless thought of as possessing an essential *unity* and *continuity*. Not only is a person considered to be unified at any one moment; a person is usually even thought to be in some sense essentially the same person that he was in the past and will be in the future. These key concepts—

actions, choices, consciousness, values, freedom, reasons, purposes, responsibility, sociality, unity—define for us a conceptual framework or word-picture of man that we shall call the image of the personal.

This personalistic framework permeates our everyday understanding of ourselves and our social relationships. Its importance can hardly be overestimated. Many of our institutions, especially the older, more tradition-bound ones such as marriage and courtship, are tied very closely to the image of the personal and would no doubt change radically or perhaps even perish were that image to cease to be regarded as true. Others, such as education, are even now in ferment as older views of the person come into question, undermining traditional assumptions about how people learn and the nature of learning itself. The concept of a person is also central to our moral traditions; to seriously abandon the personalistic framework would necessitate fundamental changes in the way we treat each other, or at the very least a change in the way we talk about and justify that behavior.

justice and the personal
Perhaps an illustration will sharpen the point. One area where the legitimacy of the personalistic framework has been sharply challenged is legal punishment. C. S. Lewis clearly perceived the implications of the controversy over twenty-five years ago and brought it into focus in his essay "The Humanitarian Theory of Punishment."[1] In this essay Lewis contrasted an older, robust view of punishment, the retributivist view, which held that criminals should be punished because they deserved to be punished, with a modern view of punishment which he termed the humanitarian view. The title is ironic because Lewis believed the newer view was anything but humane; it was, he thought, frightening. Still, the new view is apparently humane because it tries to view what used to be called "punishment" as a way of helping both the criminal and society.

The crux of the issue is that this reinterpretation of punishment as helping is purchased at the expense of the personalistic view of man. The older view explicitly presupposed that criminals were imprisoned because they were responsible agents who had made bad choices and deserved to be punished. Of course if the criminal could be helped to reform and live a better life while in prison, that was all to the good. The new view attributes the "choices" of the criminal to hereditary and environmental causes. Society has a legitimate right to protect itself from the criminal, but the notion of retribution (society "paying back" the criminal for the wrong done) is thought to be archaic and barbaric. The criminal must be understood as badly adjusted or sick. The main purpose of the criminal justice system ought to be the *treatment* of the offender. His reform and rehabilitation provide the justification for the special treatment he receives from society.

The danger of this humanitarian view is that it implicitly undermines the principle that punishment is justified only to the extent that it is *deserved*. The "treatment" which the humanitarian view wishes to extend to the criminal is just as compulsory as the old-style punishment. It still involves considerable restrictions on the freedom and rights of the individual under treatment. But this restriction of the individual's freedom can no longer be justified on the grounds that the individual deserves to have his rights restricted because of the responsibility he bears for his actions.

Since the treatment is not punishment, it no longer seems necessary to ask if it is *just* or not. If the purpose of the criminal justice system is solely the rehabilitation of the criminal and the protection of society, then the proper questions to ask of a sentence passed on a criminal are "Will the criminal be helped by these measures?" and "Will society be protected?" The fact that individuals who hold this humanitarian view of punishment do not in fact advocate unreasonable or unjust treatment of criminals does not show that the concept of justice logically coheres with their view; it simply shows that as men they are better than their theories. Punishment can be just only to the extent that the person being punished deserves the punishment. In theory at least, we punish only those who are responsible for their acts; those who are not responsible, we treat. Treatment is not punishment, and the proper question to ask about treatment is not, "Is it just?" but "Is it effective?"[2]

The implications of this issue become even graver when we recognize that treatment is only administered to the "sick." For who is sick? Who decides? Mental health and illness are notoriously value-laden concepts. Some psychologists and philosophers have believed that religion is a kind of sickness. In the Soviet Union those persons who criticize the government may be branded as sick and sent to mental asylums. The person who is committed to a mental institution is not being accused of a crime. His fate is determined by the objective medical "expert," and his "sentence" may be of an indefinite length.

Even within the field of mental health this way of treating sickness can and has led to many abuses.[3] To build the criminal justice system around these concepts could lead to far more frightening dangers. Yet it seems clear that these problems can be logically prevented only by retaining the idea that punishment must be just, must be deserved. And punishment is deserved only when the individual being punished can rightly be held responsible for the acts which he has committed. A person is responsible only for freely chosen acts; no one is held accountable, morally or legally, for doing what he could not help doing, unless his inability is caused by acts performed in the past when the person did have the ability to make a free choice.

This issue is cited only as an illustration of how crucial the personalistic framework is to the institutions and practices which bear on our treatment of human beings. It illustrates how the abandonment of that personalistic view could lead to far-ranging changes in those institutions and practices. But it is an illustration which has a special relevance to the Christian faith. For while the God of the Bible is first and foremost a God of love, he is not merely that. He is also a God of justice. He is not only a loving Father, but also a righteous judge who will hold men accountable for their actions.

Such a conception of God in his dealings with mankind simply does not make sense unless human beings are persons, agents who make free choices for which they are to be held responsible. Even the notion of a love relationship between God and man presupposes freedom—on both sides of the relationship. For love which is not freely given is not love. Is it not for this reason that God lovingly seeks man in such a non-coercive fashion, opening himself to the possibility of rejection? What we have called the personalistic conception of man is so central to the Christian faith that it is misleading to speak of it as merely a part of Christian doctrine. It is rather something which the Christian doctrines simply take for granted, something presupposed at almost every point. It is implicit in the biblical record of God's dealings with mankind from beginning to end.

the demise of the person

We have claimed that this personalistic view of man is currently under attack, and that the attack has been supported in large measure by the behavioral and social sciences. The key question which must be raised then concerns the compatibility of the scientific and personalistic views of man. Are the two really enemies? Do the contemporary human sciences really abolish the old-fashioned view of persons as responsible agents? This is a question which cannot be answered at the beginning of our inquiry, but only (if at all) at the conclusion. Nevertheless, we can say at the outset that the two views of man at least *appear* to conflict. C. P. Snow's discussion of the problem of "the two cultures" is only one manifestation of the wide-spread intellectual tension which is felt by those struggling to retain the image of the personal, without turning their backs on the intellectual advances which the contemporary sciences embody.[4]

Why is this so? At the risk of over-generalization and consciously ignoring some definite counter-movements, it is fair to say that the rise of the human sciences in the twentieth century has been marked by the demise of the person. That is, there is a definite tendency to avoid explanations of human behavior which appeal to the conscious decisions of persons in favor of almost any nonpersonal factors.

In ordinary life, for example, a convert to a religion, if asked why he is a believer might reply, "Because I have chosen to be a believer." If pressed he might offer reasons why he chose, but he would insist that those reasons were not coercive. Ultimately his own free choice is at the root of the matter. Perhaps the one point of agreement which would unite B. F. Skinner, Émile Durkheim, Sigmund Freud and Karl Marx, to take a few representative scientific giants, would be that this explanation of behavior is scientifically invalid. And it is important to see that the falseness of the believer's account does not necessarily stem from any dishonesty on his part. The problem, rather, is that the explanation does not explain; it is not a logically proper type of explanation. Beyond this these scientists would diverge.

To explain the decision to become a believer Skinner would speak of operant conditioning with its related concepts, Durkheim of the degree of social cohesion and the nature of the authority bonding the various groups which have shaped the individual's identity and world, Freud of unconscious and presumably biologically grounded forces, and Marx of the material and economic self-interests of the social class of the believer. In interpreting the explanation offered by the believer himself, such categories as rationalization, ideology and reinforced verbal-behavior would emerge. In none of this is there any recognizable facsimile of the person as a valuing, cognitively aware, responsible agent.

what makes science scientific?

Why are such personalistic categories as choices, purposes and reasons absent from these sciences of man? The answer is deceptively simple and complex. Simply, it is because social scientists have wanted to be *scientists*. The complexity arises when we try to explain how this particular conception of what it means to be scientific arose and gained widespread acceptance. One common explanation does, however, give at least part of the story: social scientists simply emulated natural scientists. Physics and biology are genuine sciences; so if we wish to be scientific we must use the methods and concepts employed by physicists and biologists. What are these methods? What makes a science scientific?

Many answers to these questions can be and have been given. Nevertheless, one particular set of answers seems to have been particularly influential to the sciences of man. This set of answers is generally associated with the philosophical movement known as *positivism*.

Though its ancestry is much older, the ideas behind the positivist movement were widely popularized in the nineteenth century by the British philosopher, John Stuart Mill, and the French philosopher, Auguste Comte. With some important changes and additions, their views lie at the heart of the twentieth-century philosophical movement known as logical positivism, which was composed of a group of thinkers who did much to advance what they called the "unity of science movement." The main idea behind the unity of science movement was simply that there is one scientific method which underlies all genuine sciences. If the social sciences wish to make progress towards that status, then they must emulate those sciences which are successful, notably physics, chemistry and biology.

The positivist view of the scientific method which is seen as underlying the success of the natural sciences emphasizes three factors. The first is empiricism, the philosophical belief that knowledge is obtained by experience. Scientific progress is made only when speculation is abandoned in favor of the quest for facts, facts obtainable only by using one's eyes and ears to observe what is happening. For the positivist, public observations, repeatable in principle, provide the final test of truth.

The second factor is an emphasis on causal explanations of an impersonal or mechanical sort. The scientist who wishes to explain an event does not ask about the purpose of the event; he abandons the quest for what Aristotle called final causes in favor of what is termed efficient causality. The scientist merely wants to understand the mechanisms underlying the natural order, mechanisms which can be expressed in the form of *laws*: "Whenever A, then B." If, by experience, we know that some law of this form is true, then we can *explain* the occurrence of B. "B occurred because A occurred, and whenever A occurs, then B occurs." If we know that some law of this form holds, we can also *predict* when B will occur, if we know that A has occurred or will occur. If our predictions hold up, then our law (regarded by some as a hypothesis) can be said to have been verified (at least in this one instance). If our prediction is wrong, then (assuming no interference from other factors) the regularity which our statement claims to hold does not hold, and our hypothesis has been falsified.

The third factor which positivists emphasize in their view of scientific method is that the scientist must employ the objective methods of logic and mathematics. To eliminate subjectivity and bias, the scientist strives, insofar as this is possible, to restrict his observations to what is measurable and quantifiable. He also attempts, insofar as he can, to express his reasoning in logical form. By these means he seeks to ensure that the facts will speak for themselves and that his work can be checked and hopefully duplicated by other scientists.

This view of science is nicely illustrated by Comte's doctrine of "the law of three stages," which is basically an interpretation of the history of science. Comte held that every science goes through three phases. Stage one is the stage of infancy or childhood in which personalistic or anthropomorphic explanations are sought for natural phenomena. Why does the thunder occur? Because Thor is angry and he is throwing his hammer. Comte also calls this the theological stage of explanation, the gods being the persons most often invoked to explain natural events. The second or adolescent stage occurs when natural events are explained by abstract principles and concepts, rather than by personal agents. At this stage the thunder is perhaps explained by a "sonic principle" inherent in storm clouds. In the mature or adult stage, the stage of "positive science," the thunder is explained by scientific laws which state the mechanical regularities discoverable in nature by observation.

This interpretation of the history of science is widespread among social scientists. It is by no means uncontroversial or unchallenged; in future chapters alternative views of science will emerge. But it has gained such currency that it is confidently offered to students who may never even have heard of Comte. For example, B. F. Skinner offers such a view in the first chapter of his best-selling book, *Beyond Freedom and Dignity*.[5] Just as other sciences have made progress by rejecting personal and abstract types of causality in favor of efficient, mechanical types of explanation, so also psychology must abandon anthropomorphic explanations put in terms of choices, purposes, reasons and so forth, in favor of empirically discoverable scientific laws. Of course, someone might observe that rejecting personal-type explanations of nonpersonal events like thunder is one thing; rejecting personal-type explanations for the actions of persons is quite another. However, to press this at this point would be to beg the important questtions. But it is precisely this point which focuses the argument between scientists like Skinner and humanists—Christian and non-Christian—who feel compelled to attempt to preserve the image of the personal.

the prestige of science

The tension between our ordinary view of man which employs personalistic categories to interpret and explain human behavior and the view of man which seems to emerge from the sciences of man is made peculiarly problematic by one other factor—the prestige of science in today's world. To be scientific is still *de rigueur* in most circles, academic or otherwise. Certainly no one wishes to be regarded as unscientific. Thus in any conflict between common sense and science there can be no question of who is right. In sophisticated circles this scientism—the belief that all truth is scientific truth and that the sciences give us our best shot at knowing "how things really are"—becomes explicit. The following quote from D. M. Armstrong, a contemporary materialistic philosopher, is representative of the tacit belief of many "tough-minded" intellectuals of a naturalistic bent.

I think that the best clue we have to the nature of mind is furnished by the discoveries and hypotheses of modern science concerning the nature of man. . . .

What reason have I, it may be asked, for taking my stand on science? . . . Why this "scientism"?

It seems to me that the answer to this question is very simple. If we consider the search for truth, in all its fields, we find that it is only in science that men versed in their subject can, after investigation that is more or less prolonged, . . . reach substantial agreement about what is the case. . . .

I conclude that it is the scientific vision of man, and not the philosophical or religious or artistic or moral vision of man, that is the best clue we have to the nature of man. And it is rational to argue from the best evidence we have.[6]

One may raise questions about this scientism, of course. Many thinkers, including many scientists, have begun to question the thesis that science provides the whole truth and the ultimate truth concerning not only man but the natural order as a whole. Their questions certainly deserve to be heard, and we shall give them a hearing in due course. Other critical questions must be raised as well, particularly concerning the nature of science. Is the view of science we sketched out in this chapter, stressing objective observation, mechanical causality and mathematical method, completely adequate? Could such methods distort or fail to reveal some of the key aspects of human persons? Is this view of science even accurate with respect to the physical sciences?

Before going on to the basic issues in the philosophy of science that these questions pose, however, it would be well to give credit where credit is due. The development of science may well be the most magnificent achievement of western culture. The prestige of science is in large measure deserved. The goal of developing the sciences of man to the level of explanatory power exhibited by the physical sciences is a noble one. The task we have set forth here—that of critical reflection on the sciences of man—must not be confused with irrational and irresponsible attacks on these sciences or on science in general.

We wish rather to pose some questions about the nature of science and the presuppositions scientists employ, with a view towards determining how, if at all, the image of the personal can be preserved in a scientific age. If our quest demands that the methods or assumptions of the human sciences be criticized, the criticisms must always be made for good reasons. The ideas we are examining are powerful, attractive and widespread. They cannot be rejected or modified without good cause.

summary and preview

Let us summarize our conclusions so far. There is a prima-facie conflict between the conception of man as responsible agent (which is implicit in Christian theology as well as much of our everyday awareness of persons) and the conception of man implicit in the dominant tradition in several of the social sciences. The depersonalizing scientific view of man seems to be necessitated by a certain conception of what makes a discipline a science, which in turn is based on a particular interpretation of the history and character of the natural sciences, emphasizing empirical observation of physical events and deterministic modes of causality. This tension is aggravated by the prevalence of scientism in Western culture, the tendency to make scientific procedures and theories the ultimate source of truth and the ultimate account of the nature of reality.

We shall now take a closer look at the scientific perspectives that seem to threaten the image of the personal. After surveying the damage, we shall try to see if there are any good reasons for continuing to believe in the image of the personal. Next, we shall examine some alternative strategies for reconciling the personalistic and scientific views of man, concluding with an attempt to sketch a contemporary model for thinking about the person in a Christian context.

minds and brains: the person as machine

2

Much of the image of the personal is bound up with the notion that persons are conscious. So one way of approaching the nature of persons is to consider what philosophers have traditionally termed the mind-body problem. That persons have bodies is fairly obvious. To almost everyone it seems equally obvious that persons have minds; they entertain conflicting beliefs, perceive colors and shapes, feel pains and pleasures, experience anguish and disgust. Diverse as these activities may be, they usually are regarded as in some sense "mental." What is not obvious is how these two obvious truths, that persons have bodies and are also "conscious," are to be unified into a coherent view of the human individual.

Arthur Schopenhauer termed this problem the "world knot," and it seems to have engaged the attention of thinkers from earliest times. It was, however, René Descartes, the seventeenth-century French philosopher, who gave the problem the formulation which continues to trouble the contemporary scientific mind.

descartes and the world knot
Descartes was impressed with the then revolutionary developments in natural science. (Indeed he contributed a great deal to those developments.) As Descartes saw it, the physical universe

was a vast machine, whose workings could be explained by purely mechanical laws. The concept that nature was purposive, or that natural events required "final causes" to serve as explanations, was to be abandoned completely. Even the higher animals, as well as the human body, were viewed as part of this vast machine. Within the created order the only exception to this mechanical world view was the human mind.

As every student taking introduction to philosophy knows, the foundation of Descartes' system was his own introspective awareness of his consciousness. "I think, therefore I am" was for Descartes the one incorrigible foundation for philosophy, the one truth which could withstand every skeptical doubt. Descartes reasoned that even if all his perceptions of the world were false, *including his perceptions of his own body*, it remained true that at least those perceptions were real as perceptions. Even if he were being deceived by a powerful, evil demon, it would still be true that he was being deceived, and therefore that *he* must exist. But if one asks who or what this self is which exists with such certainty, Descartes replies that he can only say it is a "thinking thing," a conscious substance.

This conscious substance or mind he saw as radically different from the material or "extended" stuff which composed the mechanical order of nature. Consciousness was, according to Descartes, a nonmaterial entity which engages in rational thought, emotional valuation and free choice. Human beings are then "dual," composed of two radically different substances—a physical body and a non-physical mind. Strictly speaking, Descartes identifies the person with only one of those substances—the nonphysical mind. That is, Descartes regards the true person as the soul. Nevertheless Descartes emphasizes that the soul is closely attached to a body, more closely even than a "pilot in a ship."[1]

Descartes also claims that these two different substances interact in a causal way. Physical happenings are the cause of mental occurrences and vice versa. By virtue of possessing or rather being a nonmaterial soul then, human beings were "the great exception" to an otherwise mechanistic natural order.

Descartes was obviously attempting to preserve the uniqueness of human beings. But making man "the great exception" to an otherwise mechanistic order was and still is an irresistible invitation to naturalistically inclined thinkers to eliminate this exception. The way to do this is to show that those features of human life which Descartes had viewed as mental could be explained along materialistic lines. Thomas Hobbes, the English contemporary of Descartes, produced a more thoroughgoing materialistic world view which included man within its compass. La Mettrie, an eighteenth-century French philosopher, scandalized his contemporaries with his book, *L'Homme machine (Man the Machine)*, in which he explicitly identified the mind with the brain, viewed as a physical machine.

Nevertheless, until the late nineteenth century Descartes' dualism stood the challenge fairly well. There were many problems with dualism, particularly concerning the interaction between mind and body which Descartes said took place. How could two types of reality which had nothing in common affect each other? Dualists claim that this problem is not fatal, but it led thinkers to try all sorts of curious views, including parallelism, the doctrine that mind and body have nothing to do with each other, but proceed along independent, parallel "tracks." When asked to explain the amazing correlation between mental and physical happenings, the parallelist might appeal to a divinely ordained "pre-established harmony." Bishop Berkeley, an English philosopher, tried to get rid of the mind-body problem by getting rid of matter! Berkeley argued that the only evidence we have for the existence of matter is our own subjective experience of matter. He concluded that it would be simpler (and more rational) to view "matter" as simply consisting of those experiences. Thus "to be is to be perceived"; the tree in the forest only makes noise when there is someone to hear it. (Berkeley thought God was always there to hear it.) Some of the Romantic thinkers such as the German philosopher Schelling also challenged this mechanistic view, as did Schelling's great Idealist contemporary Hegel, who tried to reject the premises which dualists and their mechanistic opponents shared in common.

three challenges to dualism
It is only in the late nineteenth and twentieth centuries, however,

that Cartesian dualism has been effectively challenged. Three views have been developed of a naturalistic character, any of which would have serious consequences for the "image of the personal" if accepted as true. These three views are epiphenomenalism, behaviorism and central-state materialism (sometimes known as the mind-brain identity theory). Two factors in particular have given these views added strength: the amazing developments in brain physiology and the construction of advanced computers—machines with "artificial intelligence." Let us examine each of these three views of the mind in turn.

Epiphenomenalism: Strictly speaking, epiphenomenalism is a version of dualism. That is, the epiphenomenalist does not deny the existence of nonmaterial conscious events. What he does deny is the thesis of Descartes that the mind can influence the body or any other physical events. According to the epiphenomenalist, all events, including mental events, have physical causes. Human behavior can in principle be explained with reference to the laws of physics and chemistry. The conscious events which we term "mind" are real, but they are "epiphenomena," by-products of the physical causes. The mind is a kind of "side show" to the real circus, which is physiological in character.

Epiphenomenalism is a congenial view for a thinker who wishes to explain all of the cosmos, man included, in materialistic terms, without requiring him to deny the existence of consciousness outright. It is perhaps best seen as a kind of compromise or halfway house between the Cartesian view of the person and a full-fledged materialism, though a compromise weighted on the materialistic side. In the nineteenth century, this view was popularized by T. H. Huxley, the English biologist who is perhaps better known to history for his defense of Darwin's theory of evolution. The Cartesian view of the person, which sees a radical break between the human person and all other animal creatures, was naturally uncongenial to evolutionists, who stressed the continuity of the evolutionary ladder.

Evolutionary thought continues to play an important role in the thinking of scientists and philosophers. But it is just for this reason that epiphenomenalism has lost a great deal of its popularity. Many reject dualism because they do not believe it to be probable that a nonmaterial mind could have evolved from a material process of evolution. Yet epiphenomenalism asserts that this is exactly what has occurred. Although he may concede that some animals are also conscious and hence refuse to draw a sharp line between man and the animal kingdom, the epiphenomenalist still admits the existence of nonmaterial conscious events which have "emerged" in the course of evolution. They may be dependent on the physical universe, but they are real nevertheless. And their existence cries out for an explanation. The hard-nosed materialist is likely to be uncomfortable with this nonphysical consciousness; it makes his scientific world very untidy.

The epiphenomenalist view is hardly congenial to the traditional view of the person either. Although consciousness is admitted to exist, it has no effect on what happens. Ideas, beliefs, fears and desires have had no impact on history. Human choices are never the result of reflection. Like most compromises, the epiphenomenalist view is not really satisfactory to either party. Nevertheless, it continues to be a popular view among contemporary thinkers, particularly physiologists doing brain research.[2]

Behaviorism: A much more radical, uncompromising, materialistic view of the person is that of behaviorism. By behaviorism we do not mean here a program or method of psychological research but a philosophical theory about the nature of mind. Behaviorism is here treated as a metaphysical position, congenial to a certain view of psychology and held by many psychologists, but not identifiable with any particular empirical psychological hypothesis. John Watson seems to have been a behaviorist in this sense; at times B. F. Skinner appears to be but his position is much more complex.[3]

According to the behaviorist the whole problem of mind and body is founded on the confused assumption that the mind is a thing or, in technical philosophical language, a *substance*. It is true that human beings are very different from other types of animals, but the dualists make a great mistake in trying to explain this difference by postulating a nonmaterial mind or soul within human beings. The actually observed differences between human beings and other animals are differences in the complexity and scope of their behavior. Talk about "the mind" is simply a misleading way of talking about some of the complexities of human behavior.

For example, one way of describing a certain piece of human behavior is to say it is "intelligent." One might say this of a person playing chess, for instance. The dualist describes the difference between playing chess intelligently and playing it "blindly" or "automatically" by claiming that the intelligent player "knows what he is doing." This seems to refer to some hidden "inner process." According to the behaviorist the fact that one person "knows what he is doing" is simply another way of talking about the particular behavior he is engaging in. That the intelligent player "knows what he is doing" is shown by the fact that his moves fall into certain patterns which finally result in victory, or at least tend in that direction. That these moves were not simply "accidents" can also be explained in behavioral terms. If the individual can duplicate his behavior by playing more chess games, if he is able to talk about the game he has played or if he is able to help another player improve his game, this shows that the player indeed "knew what he was doing." In this case, "knowing" does not refer to some mysterious inner process but to the skills and abilities of the player—skills which are definable in behavioral terms.

The dualist will insist that intelligent choices are those which are originated by the person's "thoughts." An "inner man" is postulated as the originator of the person's acts. This inner man is often derided in behaviorist literature as an "homonculus" or "little man" or as a "ghost in the machine." The behaviorist claims that the "inner man" explains nothing. Saying that a choice was precipitated by an inner "act of will" merely duplicates the outward behavior. The behavior of the real person is explained by the behavior of the homonculus, but the behavior of the homonculus is still unexplained.

It seems initially implausible to claim that mental occurrences are simply ways of referring to outward behavior, because everyone knows that a person can be angry and yet not "show it" in any external way, just as a person can be intelligent and yet act stupidly. We all remember cases where we have been forced to dissemble and hide our true thoughts and feelings; thus it does not seem plausible to identify those thoughts and feelings with behavior.

This objection is met by the behaviorist by introducing the concept of a "disposition."

A disposition can be loosely characterized as a "tendency" or an "ability." A good example of a disposition is the "brittleness" of a glass bottle. In saying that a bottle is "brittle," we are not saying that the bottle is broken, or even that it is going to be in fact broken. What is being claimed is that the bottle has a tendency to break, or that it will break in the appropriate circumstances. There are of course many of these circumstances, and it would probably be impossible to list all of the situations in which the glass would break. This does not mean that the bottle *will* in fact break; it might just be the case that none of those situations will ever occur. It would be a great mistake to think that the "brittleness" of the glass is some mysterious nonphysical property of the glass.

According to the behaviorist, mental states are similar to "brittle" in a number of ways. To say of a person that he is "angry" is to say that he has a tendency to engage in various sorts of behavior—shouting, sulking, perhaps even violence. (It is important to note that mental states typically manifest themselves in complex and various types of behavior.) It is possible that a person could be angry and never "show it," just as it is possible for a glass bottle to be brittle without ever actually breaking. To say that "Jim is angry" is merely to say that he would engage in certain forms of behavior in the appropriate circumstances. The behaviorist would attempt to give similar analyses of many other mental states. A "thoughtful" person is one who tends to respond to problematic situations in a particular way, called "reflective" rather than in other ways, less appropriate, called "impulsive."

Behaviorism as a philosophy of mind obviously seems to undermine the image of the personal. Rather than explaining behavior by referring to the consciousness of the agent, the behaviorist regards statements about consciousness to be simply oblique statements about behavior. The way is clear to explain human behavior in terms of causes beyond the control of the individual, either in the physiological make-up of the individual or in the environment. It is the latter type of explanation which is typically sought by the behavioristic psychologist.

27

Central-State Materialism: The third view of the mind which has arisen to challenge the dualistic view is central-state materialism, sometimes referred to as the mind-brain identity theory. The central-state materialist agrees with the dualist that the mind is something "inner" (and therefore differs from the behaviorist), but he disagrees with the dualist on the nature of this inner stuff. According to the identity theory, the mind is not a mysterious nonphysical substance; it is simply the brain, together with the central nervous system. Conscious events are simply physical happenings within the brain.

The central-state materialist does not, as the behaviorist does, deny the existence of consciousness. Nor is he forced, as both the epiphenomenalist and behaviorist are, to deny that mental events can play a causal role in our behavior. On this view, the reality of introspection is not denied either. When a person "inspects" his own consciousness, he is simply observing his own brain states.

For all of its strength, central-state materialism is subject to obvious problems. After all, human beings who know nothing about the brain are capable of knowing what is going on in the mind. It seems implausible, then, to identify the mind and the brain.

The materialist attempts to meet this objection and a variety of similar problems by distinguishing between the *meaning* of a statement and what a statement refers to or is about. According to the identity theorist, "lightning" and "electrical discharge" do not have identical meanings. However, a bolt of lightning *is* contingently identical with an electrical discharge, which is another way of saying that statements about lightning and statements about electricity *refer* to the same kind of thing. Not everyone knows that this is the case, however. Indeed there was a time (before Benjamin Franklin) when no one knew this. It follows, then, that it is possible for a person to know about and talk about lightning without knowing that he is in fact talking about an electrical discharge.

Similarly, talk about mind does not have the same meaning as talk about brain processes. It is therefore possible for a person to talk about the mind without realizing that he is really referring to a physical brain. It just happens to be the case that the mind and brain are identical, an identity which had to be discovered, just as the identity of lightning with electrical discharge was discovered. The discoveries which make this identification plausible are those made by contemporary brain physiologists.

The mind-brain identity theory seemingly completes the mechanistic world view. If this view can be upheld, then consciousness, "the great exception," will be absorbed into the vast machinery which constitutes the physical universe, as understood by La Mettrie's successors. The aspect of the image of the personal which seems most threatened by this view of man is the concept of free choice. If the human being is a machine, what sense can be given to the concept of free choice? Some explanation of the phenomenon termed "choice" will certainly be given, but it will not be easy to reconcile that account with the traditional view of the person.

These three philosophies of mind are in large measure rivals, although it is possible to combine them in the sense that different accounts might be given of different mental operations. Nevertheless, they are fundamentally similar in one important respect. All three suggest that the ultimate explanation of human behavior will be found in the physical laws of nature. Insofar as those laws are deterministic, they suggest that human behavior is also determined. Thus, any of the three views would seem acceptable to a Comtian determined to abolish "anthropomorphic" explanations of human behavior in favor of mechanical laws.

the brain: a thinking machine

The popularity of such mechanistic views of the person stems from two increasingly interrelated fields: cybernetics and the no less exotic field of contemporary brain physiology. Both of these fields are dominated by what has been called the "mechanomorphic" hypothesis, which is simply the hypothesis that thinking is a machine-like process. Brain researchers have proceeded on the assumption that the brain's operations are not disturbed by the activities of a nonmaterial soul or mind. Computer scientists have proceeded on the assumption that artificially constructed machines could nonetheless accomplish tasks heretofore regarded as those which required "intelligence." Thus, these two fields have moved in each other's direction, though it would be rash to speak of a merger. Brain physiologists find that computer models suggest promising avenues in understanding the brain's operations. Similarly, computer scientists increasingly turn to the brain researcher as a source of hypotheses for the construction of higher-order thinking machines.

What is meant by the hypothesis that thinking is a machine-like process? What is a "machine"? One popular answer is that a machine is a physical system which "obeys the rules."[4] That is, a machine is an entity "which operates on determinate, unambiguous bits of data, according to strict rules which apply univocally to this data."[5] This means that all machine-like processes can be described in terms of a definite sequence of simple steps. For the computer scientist, the processes must be describable in formal or mathematical terms, and it must be possible to carry them out by constructing definite, localized physical entities. (The transmission of a particular piece of instruction on a computer is accomplished via some definite physical configuration of switches, wires and so forth.)

Recent work in brain physiology has definitely proceeded on the basis of this mechanomorphic view. Brain researchers have proceeded on the assumption that mental processes are *localizable* and *specifiable*. That is, they have searched for definite physiological correlates of mental processes, and they have attempted to understand those processes in terms of definite physico-chemical sequences of events, electro-chemical in nature. And they have achieved a great deal of success. Electrical stimulation of specific regions of the brain has led to the identification of "pleasure centers" and "pain centers," which seem to produce a sense of hunger, sexual arousal, anger and aggressive behavior, fear and pain, or their opposites. Much has been discovered about the specific mechanisms which are involved in the brain's activity as well. A contemporary brain scientist summarizes the confident attitude which these discoveries imbue very well.

There are no ghosts in the brain's machinery, no unmoved movers. It is all a matter of physics and chemistry. . . . An understanding of the burgeoning brain science of our times depends on a prior knowledge of the thermodynamics of ions, membranes, and aqueous solutions. It is from an understanding of events at this level that the dawning comprehension of the entire system stems. It is only from

*this background that the nature of the nerve impulse, synaptic
transmission, and sensory transduction can be understood. And it
is a combination of these phenomena which makes the ongoing activity of our brains.*[6]

Computer scientists, and the philosophers who have followed in
their train, come at the problem from the opposite direction, but
the upshot is often the same. Rather than trying to understand
human operations as machine-like, they have attempted to view
the operations of machines as human-like. Thus, an impressive
literature has arisen which claims that it might be possible to construct a thinking machine which would legimately be termed "conscious."[7] These claims rest in part on the actual accomplishments
of computers. Computer scientists say that computers can behave
"purposefully," are capable of "learning" and do not have to do
"only what the programmer tells them." Contemporary computers
are quite capable of solving problems, improving their chess (or
checkers) game through practice and surprising their programmer. These behavioral accomplishments make it seem like an increasingly arbitrary linguistic decision to deny that computers "do
what humans do," when they are said to learn or behave "pur-
posively" or "surprisingly." There has even been serious discussion as to whether future computers might not have "civil rights."[8]

Cyberneticists, in addition to appealing to the actual accomplishments of computers, often argue on a priori grounds. One
claim made is that all empirical claims about what computers
can't do are doomed to failure. As soon as the behavior which it is
claimed the computers cannot accomplish is *clearly described*,
then some kind of mechanism which can perform the task has
already implicitly been described. Failure to produce such a
"clear" (presumably describable in formal steps) description of the
behavior invalidates the objection, since it is not clear what task
the computer has failed to accomplish.[9]

unanswered questions
Many questions arise concerning this mechanomorphic model of
mind. Both the brain researcher and the cyberneticist seem to
issue a good many promissory notes concerning what "future science will undoubtedly discover." Many have questioned the extent

to which higher mental processes are localizable. Will researchers really discover a physiological correlate to such mental events as "the sudden realization that I was wrong in fearing that a Democratic President would bring the country to ruin"? Questions for the cyberneticist remain too, particularly concerning the extent to which human thought is capable of being described in terms of formal mathematical systems. Does human perception, for example, presuppose a tacit dimension of knowledge which is not specifiable in terms of a finite set of formalized propositions?[10] The failure of "computer translation" of natural languages also casts doubt on whether verbal behavior can be duplicated by computers.[11]

These unanswered questions should not prevent us from recognizing the strength and appeal of the mechanomorphic view of mind, and the seeming outcome of such a philosophy: a mechanistic view of the person. It is unclear whether these considerations give weight to epiphenomenalism, behaviorism or central-state materialism, or are neutral among the three. But contemporary brain research and computer science seem much more congenial to one of these views than to traditional personalistic conceptions. If dualism is abandoned, can the image of the personal be preserved? If so, what changes will have to be made in our interpretation of personhood? Can the scientific findings be interpreted in such a way as to preserve belief in human freedom and dignity? These are the theoretical questions which must be faced.

Practical questions are involved as well. If the mechanistic view of the person is correct, frightening possibilities arise for the control of behavior. Brain surgery, implants and drugs present themselves as viable means of social control, means which are taken quite seriously by some. Already serious proposals have been made to control violent crime through the insertion of an electrical stimulus into a pain center in the brain. The fact that such proposals do not yet seem practical is not all that reassuring.

One characteristic of the issue is the interesting way the practical and theoretical problems interrelate. The practical problems involve ethical issues. What sorts of acts ought we to do? What sorts of acts may we do? In considering such issues, the thinker seems to adopt the traditional personalistic standpoint. That is, the ethical decision-maker assumes that he has a free choice which should be made on the basis of values which he has freely chosen after conscious, rational deliberation. If this personalistic viewpoint is to be regarded as outmoded and unscientific, then the scientist who wishes to put this technology to use would seem to be in a strange position. Can such a person, faced with an ethical decision, consistently view himself as a machine? This is a troubling question. As we shall see, similar questions occur when we wish to apply the technology gained in the other sciences that deal with human beings.

the loss of the person in psychology: freud

3

In this chapter and the next we shall consciously focus on those aspects of psychology which seem to many to be most threatening to the image of the personal. Generally speaking, this includes those schools and movements which have been most concerned with making psychology a *science*. One of these schools, behaviorism, has been much influenced by the particular conception of science we sketched in the previous chapter.

Contemporary psychology is of course a complex field. Even within English-American academic psychology very diverse perspectives can be found. When we add to this the multiple varieties of psychoanalytic theory, the picture becomes much more complex. Some of these movements, such as existential psychology, may in part support the image of the personal. But we shall ignore these views for the present. In many cases they are best understood as reactions against other views they see as depersonalizing. For now we shall take a consciously one-sided view of psychology, so as to understand more clearly the tension between contemporary psychology and more traditional, humanistic views of the person.

freud and psychoanalysis
Though it sounds commonplace, it must still be said that Freud's

impact on the twentieth-century mind has been enormous. It is really difficult for an educated person today to see the power of Freud's theories, and the changes they effected in the way persons see themselves, mainly because Freudian concepts have become so basic to our self-understanding that it is difficult to imagine how individuals saw themselves before Freud. While the scientific character of Freud's work is still controversial (many academic psychologists do not consider him a true scientist), his influence makes it impossible to ignore his work. And Freud clearly thought of himself as a scientist.

It is obviously impossible to summarize or pigeon-hole the work of a great thinker like Freud, who wrote over a long period of time and who constantly revised his views. And there are elements in his psychoanalytic theory and practice which are consistent with or even supportive of a personalistic view of man. (It is partly for this reason that psychoanalysis is unacceptable to hard-nosed behaviorists.) Nevertheless, Freud's view of the person was from the outset disturbing to many humanistically oriented thinkers and continues to be so today. And the heart of the problem is not, as many Freudians would like to think, simply that Freud's emphasis on sexuality offends people of a prudish nature. The tension goes deeper than this, and we must try to pinpoint its origin.

Indeed, it is an oversimplification to talk of a tension between Freud's view of man and humanistic views of the person. Freud's view of the person is so complex that the tension can actually be found *within* Freud. (This accounts for the divergent ways Freud has been interpreted; some of these other interpretations will be discussed in Chapter 10.) However, just as we have consciously decided to take a one-sided view of psychology so as to better understand the tension between psychology and the image of the personal, so we shall focus on one strand in Freud's thought—a strand which has been influential.

the biological basis of mind

To be brief, Freud's view of the person is fundamentally biological in origin and character. Nevertheless, his psychology is still a psychology of the *mind*. It is still mentalistic and uses certain concepts basic to the image of the personal, such as the concept of desire.

It incorporates the notion of persons as conscious beings who *perceive* the world and act so as to achieve their desires in light of their perceptions of reality. It is this which makes Freud's view so complex, and this is one factor which makes Freud's views unacceptable to behaviorists. Nevertheless, Freud's psychology, while still mentalistic, requires us to fundamentally alter our conception of the role of consciousness in the individual's total pattern of behavior, and even more fundamentally, it transforms the very notion of "mind" and "consciousness."

Prior to Freud, many philosophers and psychologists identified the notions of "consciousness" and "the mental." To say that something was mental was to say it was an element in consciousness. This view of the mind coincided happily with the Cartesian view of the person. As we have seen, on Descartes' view, consciousness is not a body or object occupying space, though it is closely linked to the body and no doubt is related to the body in various ways. From this perspective, biology could perhaps explain some bodily events, but the notion of grounding psychology in biology seemed absurd.

One of the key premises of Freudian theory is of course the assertion of the reality of the unconscious and the denial that the mind can be equated with the conscious. The mind includes elements of which the individual is not conscious, even elements which the individual cannot become conscious of, or of which he can become conscious only with strenuous effort. In asserting the existence of the unconscious as part of the mind, Freud radically changed the concept of the mental. Henceforth the mind is not seen as a transparent realm which the light of introspection can totally illuminate, but as a dark and murky realm which requires special techniques to be observed at all. Most important, the whole mind, particularly the unconscious, is seen as biological in origin and character. Instead of identifying mind with consciousness, and understanding both as distinct from the body, Freud saw consciousness as a small—and derivative—part of a mind which is largely unconscious in character, a mind whose behavior ultimately stems from forces which are biological.

Freud's training as a medical scientist was almost exclusively in the natural sciences. After three years in biology and chemistry, he spent a total of six years working in the animal physiology laboratory headed by Ernst Brücke, who was a hard-nosed materialist convinced that all animal behavior, including that of humans, could be understood as caused by systems of atoms. The influence of Brücke's materialism is clearly shown by an abortive manuscript Freud worked on in 1895, called *Project for a Scientific Psychology*. In this manuscript, which was not published until 1950, Freud attempted to give psychology a material basis by deriving it from brain physiology. The book was designed "to furnish us with a psychology which shall be a natural science; ... to represent psychical processes as quantitatively determined states of specifiable material particles."[1]

Although this project had to be abandoned, the mechanistic tendency in Freud's thought remained an important element. To the very end of his life the basic explanatory concepts Freud employs are mechanical and electrical in origin. The mind is conceived as mechanistically determined. All events, including especially such phenomena as dreams and slips of the tongue, have antecedent causes which necessarily produce their effects. The basic mechanical forces are instinctual—unconscious and clearly biological in character. These instincts are conceived basically as energy systems which seek objects upon which their energy can be released. The "cathexes" or bonds formed with these objects are not conscious but mechanical in nature. This discharge of energy can be "repressed" or "displaced" onto other objects, not only by the conscious mind, but by other unconscious forces whose existence is revealed by the "resistance" offered by the subject to the psychoanalyst's probing.

Though much of this seems merely metaphorical, Freud seems to use this mechanical language almost literally. It can hardly be purged from Freudian psychoanalytic theory without radically altering its character and robbing it of much of its explanatory value.

In his later work, Freud develops this view of the mind in terms of the three concepts of id, ego, and superego, which are understood as mental "provinces" or "structural systems." The id is the oldest region of the mind. It contains man's genetic endowment, everything that is inherited. That "everything," Freud tells us, consists largely of the instincts, which originate in the body and which are originally totally unknown to us and even in the end largely unknown.[2]

The ego, which is that section of the mind which controls voluntary movement, is really a portion of the id which has undergone a special development. The ego was originally a "cortical layer, provided with organs for receiving stimuli."[3] From this has arisen a special intermediary between the id and the external world. Whatever rationality is inherent in human beings resides here, in that part of the mind which includes perceptual consciousness, and which seeks to reconcile the instinctual demands of the id with the realities of the external environment.

A portion of the ego is in turn developed and differentiated during the long period of childhood in which the person lives in dependence on his parents. This period, Freud says, leaves a "precipitate" (note the chemical metaphor) in which the influence of the parents is prolonged.[4] As this precipitate is quite capable of opposing the ego, and as it is largely unconscious as well, Freud says it is a distinct force and gives it the term super-ego.

The super-ego is formed as a result of the "oedipus complex" (or the corresponding complex in the female) in which the young male child has a sexual desire for his mother and therefore looks upon his father as a rival. This primal desire cannot of course be fulfilled, and the conflict is ultimately resolved when the child "introjects" the father into himself.[5] By identifying the father with himself (in an almost literal sense), the child receives a kind of satisfaction of his desire for the mother. The child wishes then to be "like the father" and thus the ideals of the father (and later other authorities or "father-figures") are internalized. This, according to Freud, accounts for the development of what is called moral conscience.

Note that Freud is not merely telling us what common sense has known for thousands of years, which is that the values of children are largely derived by observing their parents. The heart of his theory, and what is genuinely novel and interesting, is his mechanical explanation of how this process of value-formation occurs.

The overall thrust of this view of the person is certain to undermine the image of the personal. Though Freud does not deny the existence of consciousness and rationality, he minimizes their importance. The basic causes of behavior are mechanistic in character and biological in origin. Our common accounts of why we behave as we do consist largely of rationalizations. Even while acknowledging the existence of consciously held values and beliefs, Freud reinterprets them as largely caused by amoral and irrational instinctual forces. Even the rational objections of critics have sometimes been written off as the product of unconscious "resistance" on the part of the critic.

freud's critics respond

Freud himself was only too well aware of how threatening his view was to the traditional view of the person. He notes that "psychoanalysis has been reproached time after time with ignoring the higher, moral, spiritual side of human nature."[6] According to Freud, such accusations are unjust. To those whose "moral sense" has been shocked and who say there must be a "higher nature" in man, Freud answers "very true." The higher nature is simply the super-ego or ego-ideal, which has been given a good explanation by psychoanalysis.

Freud's reply certainly seems to miss the point. The complaint of the humanist is not that Freud has ignored man's higher nature but that he has explained it only in terms of man's "lower nature." The problem is not that Freud has said nothing about values, but that his explanation of values seems to undermine their deep moral earnestness. A Freudian does not take values to be the expression of the voice of God as Christians do, or as the expression of the rational order of the universe as the Stoics did, or the expression of the Tao as the ancient Chinese did. Instead of the voice of God, Freud hears only the voice of the parent, mechanically internalized to resolve sexual frustration.

Perhaps a concrete example will show the difference between Freudian and traditional views of the person. Let us imagine a college student, named Robert, who has been raised in a religious home. During his junior year, Robert shocks his devout father by throwing over his faith and joining a political group committed to violent revolutionary action. The key question of course is, Why has Robert done this?

If we asked this question of Robert himself, he could give many different answers. He might say that he had rejected his faith because he no longer believed it to be true. He might cite various scientific theories which he believes are incompatible with his former religious convictions, or he might mention the attacks on his faith which he learned about in his religion or philosophy class. He might perhaps explain that as a political revolutionary, he views religion as an "opium" which dulls the revolutionary consciousness of the masses. Robert would probably also insist that, though he does have these good reasons for his choice, nothing has *determined* that choice.

Robert's explanation fits the image of the personal very well. It tends to explain acts as resulting from *choices*, which are made on the basis of *beliefs* and *values*, which may themselves be consciously reflected upon and held for good or bad reasons. Of course, Robert's account may not be correct. The traditional, humanistic account of the person does not presuppose that individuals have infallible self-knowledge. Robert may be lying or he may simply lack self-understanding. (This possibility will later be exploited as one means of trying to reconcile the personalistic and scientific approaches.) But from the humanistic standpoint, Robert's explanation is at least possibly right. It is the sort of explanation of human behavior we normally seek.

Freudian theory, on the other hand, suggests an alternate way of explaining Robert's behavior. According to Freud, religious faith is an illusion connected in a particularly close way to one's father. God is in fact a magnified father, and belief in God is closely tied to the resolution of the oedipus complex. Thus a Freudian might well explain Robert's rejection of his faith as an expression of unresolved hostility towards his father, hostility which may be totally unconscious and whose origins may lie in events which occurred when Robert was only three years old. Robert's own explanation of his behavior may well be understood as rationalization, Robert's attempt to give a plausible account which will enable him to continue to repress his awareness of the real causes.

Note that part of this Freudian explanation might be attractive to Robert himself. That is, he might well agree with the Freudian analysis of the causes of his former belief, which he now regards as an illusion. But he is likely to resist the extension of this type of explanation to his current belief. This is characteristic of reductive explanations of beliefs and decisions. They are often attractive with respect to beliefs and decisions of ourselves or other persons which we do not currently share. Our actual beliefs, on the other hand, we are anxious to regard as based on good reasons.

Note also that it does not matter whether Robert decides to believe or disbelieve. The same type of explanation can be given in either case. We can easily imagine a Robert brought up in a secular home by militant atheists who converts to religious belief; his actions could be explained in much the same way. Psychoanalysts who are atheistic will of course, like Robert himself, find mechanistic explanations of decisions to believe congenial, but will tend to see decisions not to believe as the result of rational enlightenment. A religious psychoanalyst might well see the matter differently. But once the legitimacy of this type of explanation is admitted, it is hard to see why it could not cut both ways and apply to both "Roberts." Such an explanation, if taken seriously by either Robert, could paralyze any serious consideration of religious truth claims. Of what value is the consideration of the evidence for religious belief, if my decision will ultimately be a product of unconscious needs which stem from my relationship to my father?

The point is not that the psychoanalytic type of explanation is false. We are not making any judgment as to the possible truth of either type of explanation. We are merely trying to understand the implications of psychoanalytic theory and why psychoanalytic explanations appear to undermine our ordinary understanding of our behavior.

presuppositions: the real difference
It is crucial to see that the difference between the Freudian conception of the person and the traditional, humanistic one is not merely a disagreement concerning the "facts"; that is, the differences are not merely empirical differences which could be resolved through further scientific research. Though the extent to which Freud's theories have received empirical confirmation is open to

question, and thus further research may be interesting and important, it is not likely that such research will definitively settle the issue.

The difference between Freudian and humanistic views lies at the level of philosophical presuppositions concerning the nature of man. Observations of human behavior are shaped and colored by these presuppositions. It is therefore unlikely that presuppositional differences will be eliminated simply by accumulating observations. Freud is attempting to construct a scientific psychology, and he has a particular concept of the nature of a scientific explanation. The sorts of observations of human behavior that the personalist will make, often leading to explanations of behavior in terms of *choices* which are made for *reasons*, will necessarily be discounted. *Such explanations are not the proper type of explanation.* (This type of view is even more pronounced in behaviorism, as we shall see.)

Freud himself may not have been fully aware of the presuppositions which governed his observations and interpretations. But their existence can be brought into focus merely by contrasting Freud's observations and interpretations with those of other psychoanalysts who broke with him on certain points. Ludwig Binswanger, a psychoanalyst who remained on good terms with Freud personally even while he broke with Freud professionally, has an especially clear-sighted understanding of these differences. According to Binswanger, Freud's thought represents a great achievement, a single-minded attempt to see man as *homo natura*, a natural creature whose behavior is to be explained by purely naturalistic principles. This is, according to Binswanger, a valuable "productive idea," an idea which gives us the power to discover something new and real about man. However, Binswanger himself feels that this view has severe limitations which lead to distortions as we try to understand man as a historical being, a being who values and seeks meaning.[7]

Late in Freud's life, Binswanger sent him a paper in which he paid tribute to Freud as the founder of scientific psychology but also hinted at the limitations of a scientific approach. Binswanger visited Freud, who was too ill to attend the meeting at which the paper was read, and the ensuing conversation was very revealing.

Freud seemed for a minute to concede that Binswanger's attempt to understand man's higher nature had merit. But he quickly asserted that he was not really abandoning his basic position: "Naturally, for all that you have failed to convince me. Probably our differences will be ironed out only after centuries."

Binswanger's comment on this pinpoints our chief concern in this controversy:

As can be seen from the last sentence of Freud, Freud looked upon our differences as something to be surmounted by empirical investigation, not as something bearing upon the transcendental conditions that underlie all empirical research. [8]

The difference between Binswanger and Freud is not simply one which can be resolved by appealing to the "facts." Their differences have a tremendous bearing on what the investigator is likely to count as a "fact." These sorts of philosophic presuppositions (which are not really derived from the "facts," but which, in part at least, help to determine what is to be considered a "fact") are of enormous importance in understanding both the value and the limitations of various scientific approaches to man. We will therefore keep a sharp eye out for such underlying fundamental ideas, as we continue our survey of scientific approaches to man which seem to threaten the image of the personal.

the loss of the person in psychology: behaviorism

4

The second major influence on psychology in the twentieth century which we wish to discuss is behaviorism. *Behaviorism* is a term used by many different thinkers in many different ways. At times there seem to be as many kinds of behaviorists as there are kinds of psychologists. Behaviorists do not even necessarily agree on what the various kinds of behaviorism are. It is therefore necessary to take particular behaviorists as representative of a general trend, and to add the qualification that our remarks and conclusions may be misleading if applied to other thinkers. That there *are* some general tendencies exemplified by most behaviorist psychologists is indisputable, as can be shown by comparing the writings of John B. Watson, the founder of behaviorism, with those of B. F. Skinner, the leading contemporary behaviorist.

behaviorism as science: watson and skinner

Behaviorism arose from the same impulse which we saw to be significant to Freud—the impulse to make psychology *scientific*, which meant, to the behaviorists as it did to Freud, that psychology must model itself on the natural sciences. From the very outset, the behaviorists themselves realized, as did Freud, that psychology as a natural science must inevitably conflict with some aspects of our traditional understanding of the person. In looking back over the controversy behaviorism had stirred up, J. B. Watson was quite clear about these points.

Behaviorism, as I tried to develop it in my lectures at Columbia in 1912 and in my earliest writings, was an attempt to do one thing–to apply to the experimental study of man the same kind of procedure and the same language of description that many research men had found useful for so many years in the study of animals lower than men. We believed then, as we do now, that man is an animal different from other animals only in the types of behavior he displays.[1]

Here we see that what Binswanger said of Freud seems even more true of Watson. The starting place of behaviorism seems to be a philosophical presupposition, a conviction about the nature of man, which is not so much derived from scientific observation as it is the guiding ideal and basis of the behaviorist's observations.

Watson is also clear about the tension between this guiding conception of man and traditional humanistic views of the person. *Human beings do not want to class themselves with other animals. They are willing to admit that they are animals but "something else in addition." It is this "something else" that causes the trouble. In this "something else" is bound up everything that is classed as religion, the life hereafter, morals, love of children, parents, country, and the like. The raw fact that you, as a psychologist, if you are to remain scientific, must describe the behavior of man in no other terms than those you would use in describing the behavior of the ox you slaughter, drove and still drives many timid souls away from behaviorism.*[2]

The concept of man as *homo natura* is clearly expressed here, although no doubt most behaviorists would object that Watson puts the point in a melodramatic and misleading fashion with his unfortunate comparison of humans with oxen to be slaughtered. Watson sees that the description of our behavior which many of our most significant human institutions presuppose will not be compatible with the sorts of descriptions and explorations which "science" demands.

What is this conception of "science"? It is largely the conception which we sketched out in the first chapter; it emphasizes explanations of human behavior which can be stated in the form of laws which can be tested by repeatable observations, ideally observations which can be objectively measured and quantified. These requirements, in the opinion of behaviorist psychologists rule out the "introspective" methods which were dominant in psychology at the end of the nineteenth century. The introspective psychologists had defined their discipline as the science of consciousness and had attempted to develop techniques of self-observation to gain precise knowledge of mental life. The problem with these methods and this view of psychology was that what was observed —consciousness—did not seem to be publically observable. There seemed to be no way to resolve disagreement between introspective observers. Watson, who regarded consciousness as a medieval and quasi-religious conception, simply redefined psychology as a science which studies what is publically observable. Watson's view of what is publically observable was easily expressed: "Now what can we observe? We can observe *behavior—what the organism says and does.*"[3]

Though there are important differences between Watson and Skinner, these two writers have in common a conviction that behaviorism is more than just a "methodology." There are many psychologists who content themselves with the label of methodological behaviorists. On their view, behaviorism is a useful method for studying human beings, but it does not make any philosophical claims about the nature of persons. A methodological behaviorist cannot consistently claim that his scientific work provides an account of man which is ultimate and complete (although he may claim that his science is of great value). The methodological behaviorist admits that there may be aspects of human persons which are real and important which escape his purview. Certain types of questions, certain dimensions of reality, simply cannot be pursued by the scientific method. To the methodological behaviorist this is not a criticism of scientific method, nor does it require us dogmatically to assert that these questions are unimportant, or these areas of reality non-existent. Such a methodological behaviorist will find congenial the view of science which we shall discuss in Chapter 9.

From the very beginning, however, behaviorism was to Watson more than a methodology. It was a method, but what he hoped the method would provide was a new, scientific account of human nature, which would replace "medieval," "religious" and other pre-scientific views often inherent in "common sense." B. F. Skinner agrees that behaviorism is more than a methodology, and he calls his own account "radical behaviorism" to indicate his conviction that every aspect of human life, including the "higher" activities—such as scientific thought, religious devotion, moral action and artistic creation—can be accounted for on behaviorist principles.

Skinner's behaviorism, which he describes as the "philosophy" of the science of human behavior, is much more subtle and sophisticated than Watson's.[4] Watson had little experimental evidence to draw upon and was forced to fill his books with material taken from physiology, thereby confusing the whole concept of "behavior." (Does "behavior" refer to the outward behavior of the organism or the internal physiological events within the organism?—the two are certainly not identical.) Skinner, on the other hand, with an established experimental science to draw on, consistently limits his science to outwardly observable behavior, with no confusion with physiology. Watson, heavily influenced by Pavlov's experiments with animal reflexes, attempted to explain all of behavior in terms of the concepts of "stimulus and response." Skinner notes the limitations of this type of mechanistic, "push-pull" view of the causes of human behavior, and he attempts to work with the more fluid concept of "operant conditioning," which we shall discuss in a moment.

inner mental states

The subtlety of Skinner's view stands out clearly if we compare his view of consciousness with Watson's. Watson boldly and perhaps rashly denied the existence of consciousness. He viewed thinking, for example, as simply "internal speech," which is to be explained in terms of "muscular combinations."[5] Skinner's account is much more complex, even to the point of being ambiguous and inviting a charge of inconsistency. Skinner says that the behaviorist does not so much deny the existence of feelings, sensations, ideas and other parts of our mental life as seek to clarify their nature. "Radical behaviorism ... does not deny the possi-

bility of self-observation or self-knowledge or its possible usefulness, but it questions the nature of what is felt or observed and
hence known."[6] According to Skinner, what is felt or observed is
"the observer's own body."[7] This is the small part of the universe
which is contained "within the skin of each of us."[8]

So far Skinner's position simply seems to be the view known
as central-state materialism, which we discussed in Chapter 2,
a view which simply identifies the mind with a part of the body,
usually the brain and the central nervous system. However,
Skinner also states that introspection is not a kind of physiological
research, and he says in many places that this world within the
skin is "private" in the sense that "no more than one person can
make contact with one inner world."[9]

It certainly seems strange for Skinner to say that what is observed when we introspect is our body, *and* to say that the objects
of introspection are private. Bodies are publically observable objects: even brains are private only in the sense that they are difficult to observe, encased as they are in thick skulls. Brains are in
principle observable and, in any case, persons have no special
knowledge of their own brains. A neurosurgeon operating on my
brain would be able to observe various sections of it quite well. So
it is difficult to decide what Skinner's view of consciousness
really is.

In any case, that Skinner's view of consciousness is ambiguous
is not surprising, and perhaps this ambiguity is not even very important. Although Skinner does not try to deny the "inner world"
(in fact, he says it would seem foolish to neglect this source of
information just because it is accessible to only one person), he
nevertheless does not feel any need to pay it much attention. This
is not merely because the individual's descriptions of his internal
states are never completely accurate. (They are not accurate because the verbal community, having no access to these private
events, cannot properly teach the individual how to make precise
discriminations among them.) Rather, the reason these inner
states are unimportant is that they are not the causes of behavior.

This last claim is of crucial importance and seems to go against
our ordinary self-understanding, in which we frequently explain
our behavior by referring to inner states, many of which seem to be

mental in character. "He drinks because he is thirsty." "He acts that way because he is jealous." "She ran because she is afraid." Why does Skinner believe that these inner states can be safely ignored by a science of behavior?

These explanations of behavior, according to Skinner, frequently have a purely verbal character. To say that someone is thirsty may simply be another way to say that he has a tendency to drink; to say that a person is sleepy may be to say that he has a tendency to fall asleep. Similar analyses can be given for fear, jealousy and many other mental states. Obviously, if "he is thirsty" *means* simply "he has a tendency to drink," then the statement that someone is thirsty does not *explain* the fact that they have a tendency to drink. It is just another way of asserting the same fact. Skinner believes that mentalistic explanations of behavior frequently are of a purely verbal character, as assertions about mental states can frequently be translated into statements about behavior or tendencies towards behavior.

However, not all explanations of behavior in terms of inner states are purely verbal. Skinner admits that "an organism behaves as it does because of its current structure."[10] Inner states of a physiological or psychical nature may exist as part of the causal chain which produces the behavior in question. Nevertheless, Skinner insists that these inner states are not "relevant" in a "functional" analysis.[11] First, he argues that direct information about these inner states is hardly ever available. Our knowledge of physiology is still very fragmentary; our knowledge of mental states is usually inferred.[12] (We may know that an animal is thirsty if we see him drinking or if we know he has not been given water for a long time, but we do not know it directly.) Second, Skinner notes that these inner states are useless in the control of behavior if we cannot manipulate them. "At the moment, we have no way of directly altering neural processes at appropriate moments in the life of a behaving organism, nor has any way been discovered to alter a psychic process."[13]

In any case, these inner states are not the first link in the causal chain. If an organism is thirsty, then whether thirst be taken to refer to a physiological or psychical condition, we can still ask, Why is the organism thirsty? In fact, to truly understand why the animal in question has a tendency to drink, we must know this. Animals become thirsty because of the environmental conditions of their past histories. Thus any explanation of behavior which invokes inner states still has three links: (1) an external set of conditions in the environment of the organism, (2) an inner condition of the organism and (3) the behavior of the organism. Since we must always get back to the first sort of condition, Skinner feels that nothing is lost by simply attempting to explain behavior directly in terms of environmental conditions.

We cannot account for the behavior of any system while staying wholly inside it; eventually we must turn to forces operating upon the organism from without. Unless there is a weak spot in our causal chain so that the second link is not lawfully determined by the first, or the third by the second, then the first and third links must be lawfully related. If we must always go back beyond the second link for prediction and control, we may avoid many tiresome and exhausting digressions by examining the third link as a function of the first.[14]

We can now understand Skinner's ambiguity on the nature of these inner states. Since a science of human behavior which concerns itself with "prediction and control" may safely ignore these states, their status is of little concern to Skinner. He does not feel the need to deny their existence, and he seems confident that in the long run we will have a materialistic (physiological) explanation of them.[15] In the meantime they can safely be ignored.

Mental states will play a role in a science of behavior only insofar as they can be translated into statements about behavior. (At this point Skinner is close to Watson.) Here they will function, not as explanations of behavior, but as descriptions of behavior to be explained. It is Skinner's conviction that there must be "behavioral equivalences" for expressions which refer to mental states. This is because we are taught the use of these expressions by other people. The child, for example, is taught by his mother (and others) when he is "in pain." However, the verbal community, which teaches us the meaning of these terms, has access only to our public behavior, not to any private states.[16] If this is so, then expressions like "I am in pain" can be translated into statements about behavior. Skinner does not claim that these "behavioral translations" are exactly like the originals, merely that they are adequate for scientific purposes, that is, "prediction and control."[17]

operant conditioning

To explain human behavior, Skinner employs the concept of "operant conditioning." Pavlov had called any event which makes a certain kind of behavior more likely a "reinforcer." In Pavlov's experiments, these reinforcers were paired with a stimulus. For example, when a dog sees food, there is a tendency to salivate. If some stimulus, such as a bell or light, accompanies the presentation of food, eventually the dog will have a tendency to salivate merely when the stimulus occurs. (It is important to note that the conditioned responses are merely probable.) Skinner's major contribution has been to show that this particular conditioning mechanism is not the only or even the most significant one in explaining behavior.

Skinner perceives that the organism is not simply a static object, but an active being which interacts with its environment in a variety of ways. "Reflex" actions like salivating may play a relatively insignificant role in this behavior. Hence, Skinner pairs the reinforcer, not with a stimulus, but with a response. The active organism acts or "operates" upon the environment. Some of the consequences of the organism's behavior function as reinforcers, making that particular behavior more likely to reoccur. Thus Skinner's "operant conditioning" applies not merely to reflex responses but to any behavior which the organism may perform. For example, pigeons occasionally raise their heads higher than normal. If the pigeon is fed when it raises its head (reinforced), then it can be conditioned to hold its head abnormally high.

With this powerful concept of "operant conditioning" as the basic explanatory mechanism, Skinner proceeds to develop a view of man which is far removed from the image of the personal. Skinner himself clearly recognizes the tension between his own view and traditional conceptions. The traditional view of man, expressed in the "literature of freedom and dignity," emphasizes what Skinner calls "autonomous man." This is simply the view of the person we sketched out in the first chapter, a view which emphasizes the person as a conscious agent who is at least partially

rational and partially free, and who therefore can be held responsible for both good and bad acts. According to Skinner, "a scientific
analysis shifts both the responsibility and the achievement to the
environment."[18] With consciousness disposed of, the concept of
freedom which lies at the heart of the theory of "autonomous man"
is simply not viable. Although his behavior is very complex, "man
is a machine in the sense that he is a complex system behaving in
lawful ways."[19]

Thus Skinner's view diverges far more radically from the image
of the personal than even Freud's. Though Freud emphasized the
dominance of unconscious and biologically grounded instincts, he
still accepted the reality and importance of consciousness. The ego
may be dominated by the id and superego, but it still functions as
that aspect of a person which attempts to reconcile desires with
reality. Skinner sweeps away not only Freud's ego, but the id and
superego as well. All of these "inner realities," whether conscious
or unconscious, are unnecessary for Skinner who sees man simply
as a biological organism conditioned by the environment to respond in a complex variety of ways.

a question of control
It must be emphasized that Skinner is not merely a theorist. The
goal of the science of human behavior is not merely prediction; it
is control. Since human behavior is a product of the environment,
changes in the environment will produce changes in human behavior. The science of human behavior, by experimental manipu-
lation of the environment, is aimed at predicting the behavioral
consequences of these changes. With a knowledge of these behavioral results, which Skinner calls "contingencies," the person
or persons who have the ability to modify the environment gain
the power to modify human behavior. Thus on Skinner's view a
science of human behavior is at the same time a technology of
human behavior.

Skinner believes that such a technology is exactly what is
needed to solve the problems contemporary man faces. Problems
such as the population explosion, pollution of the environment,
war, the breakdown of the educational system and the disaffection
of the young cannot be solved unless we can "make vast changes

in human behavior." And these changes can only be made if a behavioral technology "comparable in precision to physical and biological technology" is produced. Skinner himself recognizes that the prospect of such a technology is regarded by many as a cure worse than the sickness it is designed to alleviate. After all, a Skinnerian approach requires giving up belief in the cherished humanistic conceptions of freedom and dignity, and the forthright employment of manipulative techniques to induce people to behave in socially acceptable ways.

Skinner, however, feels that these objections are rooted in ignorance. Human beings are already controlled, but the control is largely invisible. Only our lack of knowledge of the causes of behavior allows the myths of freedom and dignity to survive. With a correct understanding of human behavior, Skinner says that the real problem will be seen to be not control or lack of control, but what type of control of behavior is to be exercised. Not all control is bad. "The problem is to free men, not from control, but from certain kinds of control."[20] With the employment of "positive reinforcers" Skinner claims that the objectionable features of control, which we associate with tyrannical and totalitarian governments, can be avoided. A type of control can be developed which is "free of aversive consequences."[21]

This response will hardly allay the alarms of humanists, of course, for they find unconvincing Skinner's claims about what science has shown. They may raise questions, for example, about the extent to which Skinner's empirical claims are or can be justified. But even if Skinner's claims are well grounded, problems arise.

One major problem concerns who is to exercise this control. In *The Abolition of Man*, C. S. Lewis protested that "the power of Man to make himself what he pleases means ... the power of some men to make other men what *they* please."[22] Skinner's comment on this quote acknowledges the problem but offers no hint of a solution. "This [the control of some men by others] is inevitable in the nature of cultural evolution."[23] In effect, Skinner is saying that, since control is already being exercised, the problem is not a new one. That point may be conceded without mitigating the fact that the development of powerful and effective techniques of control (assuming this is really possible) would precipitate a genuine practical crisis. To whom should this power be entrusted? Could politicians be trusted? Are social scientists to become a new priesthood? When the masses of people are being effectively controlled, the idea of democratic checks on the power of the controllers is empty. When the people possess no autonomy over against their controllers, the "will of the people" ceases to be an effective check on the actions of those controllers.

Skinner believes that these questions are not really important. As a consistent mechanist he believes that it does not matter much who the controllers are, since the controllers are in a sense "controlled" as well. This is his concept of "counter-control" (discussed on pages 84-85). But surely the slightest historical knowledge or reflection on the contemporary worldwide political scene makes it abundantly clear that it makes an enormous difference who the "controllers" of a society may be. Although the "counter-control" exercised by the "controllees" may limit the alternatives open to the controllers, vast ranges of action remain.

survival: the final value

A second troubling question concerns the ends to which these techniques are to be applied. If we had the power to change human behavior in radical ways by manipulating the environment, the question would still remain as to which changes should be made. What kind of society is truly desirable? Technological achievements do not solve the question of values; they raise new and troubling value questions. Contemporary nuclear technology makes this all too clear. Skinner himself seems to feel that a scientific analysis of behavior will not only change behavior but tell us what changes to make. Values, on Skinner's account, are simply a result of the biological and cultural evolutionary process. "Things are good (positively reinforcing) or bad (negatively reinforcing) presumably because of the contingencies of survival under which the species evolved."[24] Survival then seems to be the ultimate criterion. What makes survival more likely is good; what makes survival less likely is bad. But whose survival—the survival of the individual, of the culture, of the human race? Values which make the survival of one of these more likely may very well make the survival of another less likely.

Skinner tells us that "survival is the only value according to which a culture is eventually to be judged, and any practice that furthers survival has survival value by definition."[25] But is survival the only value? If the racist practices of Nazi Germany could have been shown to possess "survival value" for the "Aryan" culture, would those practices have been justified? Skinner has no way of telling us whether a culture should survive. If one asks why I, as an individual, should sacrifice myself to preserve my culture, or some feature of it, Skinner is surprisingly candid: "The only honest answer to that kind of question seems to be this: 'There is no good reason why you should be concerned, but if your culture has not convinced you that there is, so much the worse for your culture.' "[26] In other words, no real answer can be given to the question why a certain institution should be valued. Evolution and operant conditioning can explain why persons value certain things, but they cannot say what is really valuable. If the conditioning process has not given us a set of values already, so much the worse for us.

Skinner's view here simply will not do. The controllers who possess Skinner's behavioral technology have presumably acquired a knowledge of the environmental conditions which caused their value-behavior. With this god-like knowledge, they now possess the ability to change those conditions and presumably their own values as well. But in what directions should the changes be made? No good answer seems to be forthcoming.

This problem of values arises for the Freudian therapist as well, although here the totalitarian possibilities do not seem to be present. The Freudian view of man presents us with an explanation of why people behave as they do and why they value what they value. When the therapist judges certain forms of behavior as "sick" and attempts to help his patient become more "healthy," he is not just explaining value-behavior. He is himself engaging in the activity of valuing—the very activity on which the image of the personal puts so much stress. The psychologist, whether Freudian or behaviorist, gives more or less adequate accounts of human behavior so long as we allow him to remain an objective theorist, concerned solely with giving causal explanations of why people behave as they do. It is an open question, however, whether the psychologist can give a very good account of his own behavior as a scientist, particularly when he attempts to put his knowledge to practical use by acting upon it. Scientists too are persons and the problems posed to persons by existence must be faced by them as well.

5

the loss of the person in sociology

When compared with its status in physiology and psychology, the image of the personal has stood up rather well in sociology, anthropology, political science and the other disciplines which are sometimes grouped together as the "social sciences" in a more restricted sense. The reasons for this are no doubt various, but one important cause is that sciences which deal with man in society must at least at some point directly encounter meaningful human actions. With their roots firmly planted in real human activities—courting a potential mate, electing a public official, earning a living—these "sciences" find it hard to replace the persons who engage in such activities with subpersonal theoretical constructions. Nevertheless, the image of the personal has received some hard knocks at the hands of these disciplines as well. And it is these we wish to consider.

Our account of these social sciences will be even more sketchy and one-sided than our account of psychology because these fields are even more complex. Moreover, some of the classical writers have shown a great sensitivity to the problems we are addressing.

In addition, these fields are too broad in scope to be encompassed here. So we will first limit our discussion to one discipline—sociology—and then further limit it to "classical" theories. We shall say nothing about such recent developments as conflict theory or the neo-Marxist perspectives which have made important inroads on American sociology.

sociology as science: durkheim

The threat to the image of the personal is posed particularly by those social scientists whose view of science is largely shaped by the positivism we sketched in Chapter 1 and which turned out to be particularly significant in understanding behavioristic psychology. According to this view, genuine science always requires explanations in terms of causal laws which are empirically testable; the greatest degree of certitude is accorded to theories which can be stated in precise logical form and tested by observations which can be mathematically analyzed. A genuine social science, then, requires us to treat human behavior as a sub-class of *natural* events, to be explained in the same manner as other natural events. This is the fundamental impulse which we discerned at the heart of both Freudian and behavioristic psychology. We now will try to see what happens when this scientific ideal is applied to *society*.

Comte, with his "law of three stages," is often regarded as the founder of sociology. It is not, therefore, difficult to locate sources for the positivist thesis that a genuine science of society would eschew "anthropomorphic" explanations of social behavior in favor of the search for objective causal laws, in principle no different from the laws sought by the physicist and biologist. Besides his programmatic utterances, however, Comte did not contribute a great deal to the actual development of such a science. We shall, therefore, take Émile Durkheim as a classical representative of the trend in sociological thought which threatens the image of the personal. (We shall discuss other trends in sociology in Chapter 10.)

Durkheim (1858-1917) was a prominent French sociologist who has exercised a marked influence on the field. He stands in the tradition of Comtian positivism, particularly in his emphasis on the objective quality of social relationships and the resulting ability of the social scientist to objectively observe these relationships. (One of Durkheim's achievements was to pioneer the use of statis-

tics in sociology.) According to Durkheim the first and most fundamental rule of sociological method was to "consider social facts
as things."[1] That is, Durkheim saw social relationships as natural
objects, possessing the same sort of independence of the human
intellect as physical objects, and therefore capable of being described by objective laws, just as physical objects are. "We must,
therefore, consider social phenomena in themselves as distinct
from the consciously formed representations of them in the mind;
we must study them objectively as external things, for it is this
character that they present to us."[2] Rather than understanding
social relationships as a product of the desires, attitudes and
choices of the individuals composing the society, Durkheim believed that the study of these "social facts" would actually, at least
in many cases, explain the behavior of individuals. "Far from
being a product of the [individual] will, they [social facts] determine it from without; they are like molds in which our actions are
inevitably shaped."[3]

Durkheim's conception of sociology is well illustrated in his
monumental and historically significant study, *Suicide*. In this
work he begins with an "objective" definition of suicide. In ordinary life, a "suicide victim" is a person who intentionally, for perhaps any number of motives, takes his own life. In order to make
suicide an objective phenomenon, susceptible to scientific description, Durkheim feels he must ignore subjective "intentions." He
therefore defines suicide simply as "all cases of death resulting directly or indirectly from a positive or negative act of the victim itself, which he knows will produce this result."[4] Thus, for Durkheim's scientific purposes a religious martyr who refuses to recant
his beliefs although he knows he will be executed is a suicide victim, as is the soldier who charges an enemy position to allow the
remainder of his unit to escape, provided the soldier is aware that
his act will lead to his death. Suicide must be an objectively observable phenomenon, and, as intentions are not observable,
Durkheim feels obliged to ignore the *intentions* of the individual
committing the act.

There is of course a puzzle here: Durkheim does not really abandon the concept of "intention" in this definition. He still makes
reference to *knowledge* which the individual has of the outcome of

the act. This is significant as it illustrates how difficult it really is to describe human actions without reference to conscious intentions. This helps to explain, in my opinion, why even those sociologists theoretically committed to reductionist programs usually incorporate quite a bit of the image of the personal into their actual theories. Nevertheless, Durkheim is clearly seeking a criterion for identifying an act as a suicide which would be more objective than the individual's conscious intention.

Having given an "objective" definition of the phenomenon to be investigated, he then proceeds to seek objective causes. Suicides are to be explained, not by appealing to such factors as the beliefs or emotional states of the individuals studied but by attempting to establish relationships between the incidence of suicide and the detectable "social facts." A quote from another essay by Durkheim sums this procedure up nicely:

I consider extremely fruitful this idea that social life should be explained, not by the notion of those who participate in it, but by more profound causes which are unperceived by consciousness, and I think also that these causes are to be sought mainly in the manner according to which the associated individuals are grouped.[5]

"The manner in which the associated individuals are grouped" can of course be determined independently of the conceptions of the individuals involved, according to Durkheim. Hence, in his own study of suicide, he proceeded to correlate suicide rates with the various social groups to which individuals belong, the more important of which are family relationships, religious affiliations, political groups and economic classes. Ultimately suicide is understood as a function of such factors as the degree of social cohesiveness of the groups to which the individual belongs, and the extent to which a society fails to provide norms which regulate the behavior of the individuals (the condition of anomie).

functionalism

We are not so much interested in Durkheim's particular sociological theories here, as we are in the tendencies which his thought illustrates. Although, let us stress again, there are contrary tendencies in sociological thought which we shall discuss later, this conception of society as an objective phenomenon which "molds" the individual's behavior is widespread, and leads to far-reaching changes in human self-understanding if accepted as true. From the sociological perspective, individuals in society are hemmed in on all sides. A variety of "social controls"—legal punishments, economic sanctions, peer-group pressure—restricts the individual's freedom of choice within very narrow limits. Social institutions, such as the law, education and the family, are not invented by the individual. They are in relation to him as objective as the laws of gravity, and in many cases they have even more to do with limiting his sphere of choice.

Peter Berger, a sociologist who has a great deal of sensitivity to these problems, sums up this powerful view of man in society well: *Most of the time the game has been "fixed" long before we arrive on the scene. All that is left for us to do, most of the time, is to play it with more or with less enthusiasm. The professor stepping in front of his class, the judge pronouncing sentence, the preacher badgering his congregation, the commander ordering his troops into battle –all these are engaged in actions that have been predefined within very narrow limits. And impressive systems of controls and sanctions stand guard over these limits.*[6]

One way in which this Durkheimian perspective has worked itself out has been in the pattern of explanation known as "functionalism."[7] This type of view, which has been employed in various ways in anthropology as well, consists in viewing a society as a working system which can be analyzed independently of the beliefs of the members of the society. The social institutions are explained with reference to their functional value in maintaining the society, regardless of whether those functions are understood by the participants.

To use a crude example, let us suppose that a certain tribe which practices polygamy believes that this pattern of marital relationships is mandatory because it has been commanded by the local deity. A sociologist (or in this case rather an anthropologist) giving a functional analysis would look for a different type of explanation. He might note that the tribe is constantly engaged in wars with surrounding tribes and hence that there is both a continual need to replenish the population and a shortage of males, due to the continual bloodletting. In such a situation, the scientist might point to the functional value of polygamy in meeting these needs as the true explanation of the practice, even if the members of the tribe have no understanding of this function.

In sociology this functional analysis is often expressed by looking at social institutions in terms of their "manifest" and "latent" functions, concepts developed by the American sociologist Robert Merton. The manifest functions of a social institution are the functions the institution consciously is designed to fulfill; the latent functions are the underlying functions which may be totally opaque to the participants. Thus a sociologist analyzing the individualistic moral teachings prevalent among a certain religious group might claim that one of the "latent" functions of defining evil in terms of *individual* sins like fornication, swearing and drunkenness might be to prevent undue anxiety over various forms of *social* injustice, such as racism, which are rampant in that society. Thus, a definition of sin as purely individual might have functional value to a group which benefits from racist practices.

ideology

One might in cases like this inquire about the status of the individual's own explanation of his actions. What about the conscious motives and beliefs of the members in society? Very frequently the sociologist treats these phenomena, not as explanations of behavior, but rather as more behavior to be explained—social phenomena to be accounted for in much the same way as other phenomena. Frequently, the concept of "ideology" is employed in this respect.

The concept of "ideology" functions in much the same way as the concept of "rationalization" does for the Freudian psychologist or the concept of "reinforced verbal behavior" does for the Skinnerian. For the Freudian, although the true causes of behavior lie beneath the surface in unconscious instinctual forces, the individual nevertheless must make his behavior seem intelligible to himself and others. Hence he manufactures an account of his behavior, a rationalization. This is not a lie; the process of producing the rationalization is also an unconscious one, and the rationalization will not be effective if the individual does not believe it himself.

Similarly the Skinnerian who explains a piece of behavior in terms of operant conditioning must give some account of the "reasons" the individual involved would give for his behavior. The solution is simply to treat the individual's activity in giving his reasons as one more piece of behavior—in this case verbal behavior—to be explained by the same principles of operant conditioning. The individual gives a certain account of his behavior because that particular response has been reinforced by the verbal community.

In much the same way, sociologists speak of "ideology" in explaining beliefs of a society, particularly those beliefs which serve to justify or legitimate institutions which have a functional value not obvious to the participants. This is particularly true where the functional value of the particular institution involved lies in maintaining the special status or position of some particular class or group. The concept of ideology has been employed to a great extent by Marx and by Marxist thinkers, who are keenly aware of the extent to which beliefs may function as rationalizations of economic self-interest. But the concept is widely employed by non-Marxists as well, in both economic and noneconomic contexts. Ideology is in these cases often viewed as a kind of self-deception, which is by no means to be identified with lying or conscious hypocrisy. The ideologue is a person who believes his ideas, however distorted those may be. Sociologists frequently employ the concept to refer not merely to political or religious belief systems of a comprehensive sort but to more mundane beliefs such as the physician's conviction that the fee for service system produces the best medical care or the undertaker's conviction that an inexpensive funeral shows disrespect for the dead.[8]

In this discussion of ideology, we have gone beyond our original description of individual human behavior as molded by objective societal forces. Describing the individual as molded in this way implies that the individual and society are external to each other, with one restricting the other. Society limits the individual, but the individual has some degree of independence. But if human beliefs are shaped by societal forces, then this picture is misleading. The individual is not an autonomous unit who bumps up against an objective structure. For the most part he does not bump up against that structure, since his own beliefs—including his value beliefs—have been shaped by that structure. And "the individual" to a great extent is identical with his beliefs.

This type of sociological analysis can easily be applied to other aspects of the individual's personality as well, particularly his desires and wants. From this perspective the "individual" is largely if not completely *constituted* by the "social roles" he plays. He is not merely limited to choosing among predetermined "roles"; even his choices will reflect the roles which he has assumed, or which have been forced on him, whether those roles be economic, racial, familial or whatever. The sociologist here tries to answer the question of personal identity by understanding the person as formed by his society.

When the central beliefs and values of individuals are regarded as causal products of impersonal societal forces, then the conception of the person as a valuing, rational agent has suffered a severe setback. The individual may claim that he acts as he does because of his beliefs about the ultimate nature of things. He refrains from stealing because it is against the natural law, or God's commands, or the individual's "moral sense." The sociologist will cheerfully explain his behavior in a quite different manner, even including the individual's "good reasons" as part of the data to be explained. Such a perspective on human behavior requires a staggering "relativisation" of beliefs and values. What is "right" and "true" depends upon what culture and group within a culture one belongs to. Of course, sometimes individuals change their beliefs and values, as do societies. But the mechanisms whereby this occurs are just that—mechanisms.

the question of values
If this sociological account of the formation of beliefs and values is absolutized, as is done by some in the field of "sociology of knowledge," it leads to some interesting problems. Although many sociologists may simply be interested in understanding human behavior for its own sake, most are interested in the potential usefulness of sociological knowledge. A knowledge of social mechanisms may not only give us more understanding; it may also help us to design a better society. But if *all* values are viewed as relative products of social conditioning, it is difficult to see how a particular vision

of society can be genuinely believed to be "better." And if *all* beliefs are explained as a result of social conditioning, must not this apply to the beliefs of sociologists as well? The sociologist who continues to be a person then faces problems similar to those faced by the mechanistic brain scientist or the Freudian and Skinnerian psychologists.

As we have repeatedly stressed, we are not here trying to decide the truth of this view of the person. Questions of empirical verification of such perspectives can and should be raised. It may be significant that sociological theories do not have the sort of universal acceptance of, say, Newton's laws two centuries ago. Furthermore, the picture we have painted of "sociological man" is sketchy and one-sided. A fuller picture would contain elements sympathetic to the image of the personal, as well as other troubling elements. Some filling in of the picture will be done in Chapter 10.

Nevertheless, the way in which the sociological perspective is threatening to the humanist should be clear. Admittedly the sociologist's supra-personal structures do not seem as threatening as the biological models of man which seem dominant in psychology, or the mechanical models of the cyberneticist. These social forces appear more vague and elastic; perhaps they will bend enough to allow individuals room to breathe. But the basic thrust is clearly against the image of the personal.

With more space and knowledge we might extend this analysis to the other social sciences: anthropology, political science, economics. In all of these areas we would find a mixed picture, as in sociology, with some tendencies which support or at least do not threaten the image of the personal. In some fields these tendencies are stronger than in others. For example, much of the classical work done in cultural and social anthropology seems very humanistic. But in all the social sciences which consider themselves *sciences*, and understand science as the search for empirically testable laws which explain the data in question, the image of the personal is under fire, and in many cases, very much on the defensive.

6

feeling the loss: why care?

Having completed a brief excursion into the scientific realms which seem most threatening to the image of the personal, it is now time to treat with some seriousness the problems posed by abandoning the traditional view of the person. In exploring the ways in which scientific accounts of man threaten the image of the personal, our purpose has been neither to condemn nor defend such accounts. The fact that the acceptance of a scientific view of man would be painful is no argument against it. No fair-minded observer would deny that contemporary physiologists, cyberneticists, psychologists and sociologists have added immensely to human self-understanding. To the extent that these scientists offer us truth about the human condition, nothing will be gained by denying or ignoring that truth. Nevertheless, before abandoning a personalistic view it would be well to take stock of just what one is being asked to give up.

At the conclusion of each chapter dealing with the development of scientific views of man, we noted certain problems which arose. In this chapter we shall explore those problems in more depth.

Personalism may in the end simply be false, in which case any honest thinker ought to give it up regardless of the cost. But before we do so, we should try to determine why humanistic thinkers believe that the battle for the person is one worth fighting. Such a preliminary understanding of "what is at stake" seems especially important in an area where scientific evidence and philosophical presupposition are so closely intertwined. It is possible that some sort of truce can be worked out which will preserve the legitimate claims of both the personalistic and scientific conceptions, either through reinterpreting the message of science or reinterpreting the image of the personal—or both.

In the first chapter we stressed the importance of personalism to the Christian thinker. This, however, does not mean that the concerns dealt with here are narrowly religious or parochial. Many non-Christian and even nonreligious thinkers want to preserve the concept of the person as a conscious, valuing agent.[1] Christian and non-Christian humanists can find a great deal of common ground here.

agents, events and acts

The core of the image of the personal as we outlined it in Chapter 1 is the concept of *agency*. Persons are beings who *act*. To understand the importance of that assertion it is necessary to explore the concept of action, a subject to which philosophers have devoted a great deal of attention in the last few years. Although an act is a type of happening or event, it is not a mere event. That is, though all actions are events, not all events are actions. What is the difference?

Events are changes of some sort. When something has changed, or there has been an "occurrence," it is appropriate to ask, "Why did it happen?" That question is typically a request for a causal explanation. What event(s) preceded and brought about this event? Typically, an event is explained by subsuming it under a known regularity, which in the case of science takes the form of a law. B happened because A happened, and "whenever A, then B."[2]

Let us imagine that a child playing on a hillside is injured by a falling piece of rock. This might serve as a paradigm of an event. Let us imagine that the boulder was simply loose and, as boulders on steep hillsides are prone to do, came tumbling down. It makes perfectly good sense to ask for an explanation of the occurrence. That explanation might be that recent heavy rains had loosened the rock, or it might simply take the form of pointing out the steep slope of the hill and the plenteous number of loose rocks on it. Such explanations presuppose knowledge of such regularities as those embodied in the following statements: "Heavy rains resulting in loosening of rock piles frequently result in rock slides" or "Steep slopes covered with rocks frequently produce rock slides." Generally in ordinary life these regularities are so well known that they are simply assumed.

A "mere event," however, is quite different from an act. If we assume that someone performed the act of pushing the boulder that hit the child, a host of new questions emerge. First of all, one may ask, "Who did it?"—a question which does not emerge in the case of an event. And although the question "why" will be asked again, it is likely to require a different answer. Typically, in the case of an act, to ask "why" is not simply to ask, "Why did it occur?" but "Why did so-and-so do it?" That is, what is being requested is not a simple, causal explanation of the event, but an account of the reasons or motivation of the agent. Other questions will be relevant as well. Was the act intentional? If so, what was the agent's intention? Was he trying to hurt the child? Or was he simply amusing himself by watching rocks tumble down the hillside, unaware of the child's presence?

Two concepts are especially bound up with the notion of an action: the concept of responsibility and the concept of an intention. An act is an event for which it makes sense to ask, "Who is responsible?" It would be out of place to talk of responsibility in the case of the "natural" rockslide, except in a purely causal sense. No one would *blame* a rock for falling down a hillside. Unless the slide is the result of someone's act or failure to act (as might be the case if a strip-mine company had not properly restored the area after mining it), then it is not an event for which we seek to determine responsibility. In the case of an act, however, we not only hold someone causally responsible, but frequently responsible in a moral and/or legal sense.

In determining this moral or legal responsibility and whether the agent is entitled to praise or blame, the *intention* behind the act becomes significant. Actions generally have a purposive quality, and the purpose is not simply a byproduct of the act; it is essential to understanding the nature of the act. For example, an accidental stabbing and a murder could in some circumstances be physiologically indistinguishable. The difference between the two acts might lie purely in the intent or lack of intent on the part of the agent.

Explanations of an act in terms of "reasons" differ significantly from causal explanations.[3] Although a reason may be viewed as a type of cause, citing someone's reason for performing an act is not like appealing to an observed regularity of nature or a scientific law. It does not explain the act by showing its inevitability or likelihood, given the antecedent conditions, as a scientific causal account would. It rather is an attempt to make the act intelligible by explaining its point or purpose. Understanding the agent's reasons for acting does not always mean that one understands why the act was inevitable, because the act may not have been inevitable. It is quite possible that someone else might have the same reasons to perform the same act and yet fail to do so, either because the second person "lacked the will" or perhaps because he judged the act to be morally wrong. Thus, we can understand the point of the action of a man who steals bread for his family. The act may be seen as intelligible, even defensible, without being seen as inevitable. Another person in the same situation might have the same reason for acting and nevertheless refrain.

Thus an action does not have to be understood as causally determined to be intelligible. And an act which is not causally determined is not necessarily uncaused. "Having a reason" seems to be a kind of cause which does not necessitate. This feature of actions is crucial. It is only in those cases where an agent's choice is regarded as at least partially free that we are entitled to hold him responsible for his action in a moral or legal sense. If an airplane pilot's engine shuts down through no fault of his own, no one would hold the pilot responsible for the resulting crash. A plane crash which is the result of a failure to execute safety checks would be quite another affair. In general no one is held responsible for doing what he could not do, or not doing what he could not help doing, unless the person's inability is the result of a previous free choice.

A person who is engaged in "making up his mind" or deliberating about what he should do is engaged in a very special kind of activity. *Deciding* what one is going to do differs greatly from *predicting* what one is going to do. Although causal knowledge will be valuable to the decision-maker in the sense that such knowledge enables him to anticipate the likely results of various alternative courses of action, to make his decision the person will be interested in "data" of a different sort. He will seek to understand which of the alternative courses of action is *better*, and why it is better. He will have to decide what he considers to be really important and significant. His attitude is not that of the detached spectator who observes his past choices and attempts to predict how he will choose in this instance. Insofar as the agent is really deliberating, he cannot regard his act as an already determined fact. He is not trying to guess or predict what he will do, but to decide what he will do.

A person is then someone who makes decisions or choices, and it is crucial to our understanding of persons that they are seen as sometimes free in the sense that there are various possibilities which they could actualize. These free choices can be explained, in the sense that the agent's reasons for acting can be disclosed, without eliminating this free character. Although it is possible to assert that this freedom is limited in the sense that the possibilities for action may be restricted and weighted, it cannot be eliminated without eliminating the concept of personhood as we have outlined it. It is not necessary to believe that a person's choices are always free to preserve the image of the personal, but it does seem necessary to believe that they are sometimes free.

If freedom is eliminated, then the distinction between an action and a mere event disappears, or at least the significance of the distinction seems to vanish. To assert that human actions are determined in the sense that they conform to experimentally derivable causal laws is simply to regard them as "mere events" which are part of the natural order. If the distinction between an act and a mere event does not hold, then explanations of human behavior in terms of "reasons" would seem to be a pointless exercise. These sorts of explanations are not equivalent to explanations by causal laws. Nor would the activity of deliberating or deciding what to do seem to have much point. It would seem more appropriate to attempt to *predict* one's future actions on the basis of past experience, just as one does not attempt to *decide* what a rock falling down a hill will do, but rather attempts to anticipate or predict its behavior.

It seems, then, to be an essential feature of our concept of personhood that persons are seen as to some degree transcending the "order of nature." This is often expressed by speaking of the person's autonomous or self-determining character. Human beings are not just *products*; they have a hand in shaping themselves. In speaking of the person as autonomous or transcendent, we must add certain qualifications. First, it must be clear that this autonomy or transcendence is relative and partial in character. No one can deny that the person is also a part of the natural order, even if he partially transcends that order. Persons may be agents or producers of actions, but they are also products—of their heredity and environment, both natural and "cultural."

Second, speaking from a Christian standpoint, we must make clear that this autonomy or transcendence is in relation to nature, not to God. We are not asserting that persons are self-creating or that they are "the foundation of their own freedom," to use Sartre's phrase. If persons are transcendent or autonomous, their transcendence is itself a gift from God, not a quality that human beings have achieved on their own. Freedom is limited by God's sovereignty and is only made possible by the mystery in which God "steps back" from his creation and gives to it a limited independence. Though humans may have something to say about "shaping themselves," from a Christian standpoint they play out this role in dialogue, not only with their fellow humans but with their Creator.

We will now attempt to focus more closely on the implications of the denial of human transcendence for three areas: epistemology, morality and political theory. In each case we will attempt to show how the image of the personal is intimately bound up with meaningful human activity, spelling out the implications of rejecting a personalistic understanding of ourselves.

epistemology and the loss of the personal
The mechanistic world view requires us to abandon the conception of man as autonomous or transcendent of the natural order. Hu-

man beings are simply part of the great machine, and their behavior differs from the behavior of other natural objects not in kind but only in degree of complexity. This is best expressed by the claim that all human behavior is explainable by deterministic laws, in which specifiable conditions will always produce a specified outcome. The chief support for this viewpoint comes from the sciences which, with some success, treat human behavior as lawful in this sense.

Insofar as mechanistic claims are rooted in science, they are logically tied to certain canons of rationality. The claim that a certain proposition ought to be accepted as scientifically accurate is a claim that this proposition has received rational grounding. This rational grounding consists of evidence (in the case of science, generally experimental data) which supports the particular proposition in question, either positively or by casting doubt on the alternatives. Science, then, is a normative enterprise in the sense that the scientist does not merely give us causal explanations of why he accepts certain propositions but *reasons* for accepting certain propositions. Science cannot afford, therefore, to be indifferent to the concerns of epistemology, that area of philosophy which concerns itself with knowledge and the justification of claims to knowledge.

Science is a human activity, and a description of the behavior of scientists is quite similar to the description just given of an action, rather than a mere event. A scientist who tries to decide which of two alternative hypotheses to accept is an agent deliberating about what he is to do. In making his decision he weighs the evidential *value* of the rival hypotheses. He assumes that his decision is free and uncoerced. For him his own decision is not a future event to be predicted but a choice to be made. If someone asks why he chose a certain hypothesis, he will offer a logical justification of his choice, not a psychological explanation of it. That is, if someone asks, "What *caused* you to choose hypothesis A?" he will answer by citing the evidence for hypothesis A, rather than by citing experimentally grounded psychological laws about the behavior of scientists. The scientist does not merely tell us why he in fact accepted the hypothesis (though he does do that); he tells us why the hypothesis *ought* to be accepted.

So far we have attempted to show that the behavior of scientists is usually understood in personalistic terms. If science, viewed as a human activity, presupposes that scientists are persons in the sense we have outlined, it will be difficult to see how one could reject personalism on the basis of science. But to make the case for this, it must be shown that the mechanist cannot account for scientific activity in his own terms, which is seemingly a tall order. It is always difficult to show that it is impossible to do something. Perhaps, though, we can at least make it clear why the mechanist has difficulty accountihg for rational activity, and why it seems *unlikely* that he will be able to give a coherent account of this feature of human behavior. The argument we will employ is taken from Lewis White Beck's book *The Actor and the Spectator*, although the germ of the argument can be found in many writers.[4]

To show the difficulty of giving a mechanistic explanation of rational activity, we will introduce the concept of a "self-stultifying assertion." A self-stultifying assertion is not a logical contradiction, but an assertion no one would ever have occasion to accept, because the conditions surrounding its assertion undermine its claim to truth. An example would be the famous "liar" paradox. The assertion "I am telling a lie" could never be rationally accepted, because the assertion, if true, undermines itself. Note that this assertion is only self-stultifying in its first-person present tense form. "He is telling a lie" and "I told a lie" are perfectly acceptable. What I wish to claim is that the assertion, "I am a machine" is also self-stultifying when uttered in the first-person present tense.

Suppose some person, let us call him Jim, asserts some proposition "P." The question is then raised as to whether I should accept this proposition which Jim has asserted. Let us suppose for a moment that Jim is a machine in the sense that his behavior is describable in terms of deterministic laws. On this assumption, I am much less likely to accept "P" than I would be on the assumption that Jim is a free, rational agent. If Jim is a machine, I can meaningfully ask for an explanation of his assertion, but this explanation will be a causal explanation of why he did in fact assert "P," not a rational account of the evidence for "P." *And this sort of causal explanation of Jim's behavior could be given, regardless of whether "P" is true or false.* The fact that Jim's behavior can be causally explained is no reason by itself for us to believe "P" is true.

In ordinary life, whenever I have reason to think that a person's assertions can be explained purely by reference to nonrational causes, I immediately put less stock in those assertions. For example, suppose it should be discovered that whenever someone takes a certain drug he begins to believe that he has the power to fly through the air. In that case we could give a causal explanation for his belief, but that explanation would not be a reason for accepting the belief. In general, beliefs which can be explained by bone tumors, "brain-washing" (if such a phenomenon truly exists) or any other nonrational causes tend to lose credence. The beliefs of a person which are caused by taking LSD may still be true, but if we know that his beliefs are a product of nonrational causes rather than a free weighing of evidence, then we are less likely to give the individual's opinions weight.

These considerations hold true in the case of Jim as well. If Jim is a machine, then his beliefs can be explained by causal laws, but an explanation of why Jim in fact holds his beliefs is not an explanation of why those beliefs should be accepted. Of course Jim's assertions may be true, but the fact that Jim asserts them is not in itself a reason to accept them as true, since his assertions are not governed by rational criteria. The fact that "Jim asserts P" would be a reason for accepting P only if we, as a matter of fact, had discovered by experience that Jim's assertions were usually correct, which could in fact be the case. Supposing Jim is a computer, our faith in the reliability of Jim's conclusions would be in large measure based on the past reliability of Jim and other similar computers. If Jim is a computer, an additional factor in favor of accepting Jim's assertions might be our faith in the designers of the computer, whom we regard as rational agents, sensitive to rational criteria, who engineered the machine in such a way as to produce true results.

We might then in certain cases be justified in accepting the testimony of a machine, particularly where we have evidence for the proposition, "This machine is likely to produce true assertions." Thus, I accept the machine's testimony because I have good reasons for doing so. *I cannot regard myself as a machine in this case, however!* Although I might in certain cases be justified in accepting the "testimony" of a machine, my ability to make that judgment presupposes that I am not a machine. When I decide to accept the evidence for the reliability of the machine, or any other evidence, I do not do so on the basis of a causal law which describes my behavior, but on the basis of rational criteria which I am free to respond to in appropriate ways. If someone succeeded in explaining my behavior in accepting the proposition "Jim is a truthful machine" on the basis of some such law, that would constitute an account of why I in fact accepted the proposition, but it could never amount to a reason for accepting it. If someone *proved* to me that I had not accepted the proposition on the basis of rational evidence, I should immediately lose faith in my own belief (and incidentally, my ability to evaluate the proof as well). I conclude that the proposition "I am a machine" is self-stultifying, because if true, my assertions are not governed by rational considerations and I have no reasons to think my assertions are true, including the assertion "I am a machine."

The germ of this argument can perhaps be put more simply by noting that my belief about the causes of my beliefs is one of the factors which affects what I believe. Imagine a person who has been convinced that his beliefs on a certain topic are the result of physiological changes in his body. Let us imagine, for some bizarre reason, that eating cream of wheat cereal every morning produces a belief in him that the Russians are planning to mount an atomic attack on his city. As soon as the person accepts the idea that there is no rational basis for the belief, but that it is in fact caused by this physiological change, the belief would tend to be undermined. To recognize that a belief has *only* a causal and no rational basis tends to nullify the belief in question. And this is so whether the causes be changes in the brain, biological instincts, environmental conditioning or societal structures.

When we examined the sciences that deal with man, we found a tendency to disregard the *reasons* individuals adduce for their beliefs in explaining cognitive behavior and a tendency to favor objective causal laws. The reasons individuals give for their beliefs are typically regarded as "rationalizations" or "reinforced verbal behavior," to be explained in the same way as other human behavior. The question which must be posed now is whether the scientist dealing with human beliefs can apply this type of analysis to his own beliefs as a scientist without undermining the force of his conclusions.

Some have tried to do this. B. F. Skinner, for one, has attempted to apply his account of behavior as determined by operant conditioning to his own behavior as a scientist.[5] Skinner attempts to give an account of how the scientific community reinforces certain assertions and through "negative reinforcement" extinguishes others. However, it is hard to see how Skinner's account can be anything but a causal explanation of why he in fact holds certain views. Such an account can never amount to a reason for accepting those views, unless we assume that the community which does the reinforcing is a community of free agents, sensitive to rational criteria.

Similar analyses could be carried out on a physiologist who tries to explain his acceptance of propositions about the brain as a result of causal laws which describe his brain processes, or on the Freudian psychologist who has the temerity to regard his own beliefs as a result of unconscious instincts, or on the sociologist who attempts to explain his acceptance of certain sociological theories on the basis of the economic interests of the class to which he belongs. All of these accounts may function very well as causal explanations of why the scientists in question might hold these theories, but they hardly amount to rational justification of the theories in question. For the scientist to accept such an account of his own behavior amounts to admitting that his work is not scientific in character, as it is not governed by rational criteria.

morality and the loss of the personal
The second major difficulty for the mechanist is accounting for moral activity or, more broadly, the behavior of persons as valuing beings. The mechanist has no difficulty giving causal explanations of why certain acts or results of acts are valued. However, by explaining this valuing activity as solely the result of nonrational, deterministic laws, the objective validity of those values is called into question.

The pattern here is analogous to the problem faced by the

mechanist in explaining cognitive activity. The mechanist can explain cognitive activity, but his explanation tends to destroy faith in the rational validity of that activity. Hence if he applies his analysis to his own arguments, these arguments lose their force. Similarly, the mechanist who applies his causal account of values to his own activity as a valuing being, tends to undermine his own belief in the objective validity of those values.

This is again a "first-person problem." It does not really arise as long as the scientist is purely an observer of other human actions—a pure theorist attempting to give causal explanations. The problem is first felt when the attempt is made to put scientific knowledge to use in some way. That scientific knowledge of human behavior is potentially useful is usually strongly insisted upon by its proponents, and there seems to be no good reason to doubt this contention. With an adequate knowledge of the mechanisms governing human behavior, the scientist (or the politician relying on the scientist) gains the ability to predict the outcome which will result from particular situations and practices. With this predictive ability, the scientist can then intervene to change those outcomes by making selected changes in the "variables," provided of course that he has the practical power or ability to effect those changes.

The problem arises when the individual who has the power to effect such changes asks himself, "What changes should I make?" Granted that a person has the power to make a better society, that power is of no use if he cannot believe that some form of society would be truly better. But can the mechanist believe in objective values?

The difficulty begins when the mechanist attempts to give explanations of value behavior which understand values to be the product of essentially impersonal, nonrational causes. Such explanations of values invariably involve a relativisation of the values explained. The Freudian who explains values on the basis of unconscious mechanisms, the Skinnerian who views values as the result of operant conditioning, the sociologist or anthropologist who views values as the result of cultural shaping and the brain scientist who sees values as the result of one's genetic inheritance are all giving explanations of why people *hold* certain values. But none of these explanations give any reason to think that those values are indeed genuine values.

This essentially relativistic standpoint seems fine as long as one is simply observing and explaining the behavior of others. The difficulty arises when these explanations of values are applied to one's own values. A person who chooses one act over another because he believes it to be better must believe that it really is better. He does not merely want a causal explanation of why he *believes* it to be better. He wants to understand why the act *is* better. He is seeking a reason to choose one option over another, not an explanation of why he will in fact choose one option. Seriously to believe that one has chosen a certain option, not because it is genuinely better, but because one has been causally conditioned to regard it as better, amounts to giving up one's belief that the option is really superior.

This is another case in which a person's beliefs about the causes of his beliefs influence those beliefs. To go on believing in the objective validity of certain values, while at the same time accepting the thesis that one has no good *reasons* to accept those values but has merely been conditioned to hold them, is an instance of the sort of self-deception Jean-Paul Sartre calls "bad faith." Once one has "seen through" values and regards them as natural products of evolution, instincts and so forth, it is irrational—and psychologically difficult—to go on regarding those values as objectively valid. One's values might still be genuinely worthwhile, but one would have no reason to think them so, or at least no reason to think that one holds them for any good reasons.

Sometimes serious attempts are made to evade this problem. Periodically we hear calls for a "scientifically grounded morality." B. F. Skinner, in fact, is a good example of a thinker who makes such an attempt. Skinner claims that a behavioral science cannot only tell us how to change behavior but what changes to make. "Things are good (positively reinforcing) or bad (negatively reinforcing) presumably because of the contingencies of survival under which the species evolved."[6] Thus when we call something good or bad we "classify it in terms of its reinforcing effects."[7] Skinner believes that experimental study of the "contingencies" which affect human existence will give us the ability to perform this classification with more accuracy.

Skinner's account of values is typical of those offered by mechanists. It can be taken in two ways, both of which fail in their purpose. It might be thought that Skinner is merely giving us a causal account of why people hold certain values, an account which explains values as the result of natural selection, operating both in the life of the species and the individual. If so, Skinner has not shown us why these values ought to be accepted. He has stated the causes of their acceptance, but has not given us reasons for accepting them.

Only when we presuppose the validity of certain values does Skinner's account begin to look like a justification of certain values. Given some criterion of value, we might, through experimental tests, determine whether certain acts are likely to lead to favorable outcomes. In *Beyond Freedom and Dignity* Skinner seems to presuppose survival as the ultimate value. Whatever contributes to survival (whether of the individual, culture or human race is not completely clear) is good. If we agreed that survival (or some other good) is the ultimate value, Skinner's procedure would make sense. But his experimental ethics would not justify this ultimate value; it would presuppose it at every step. And it is by no means obvious that mere survival is the ultimate value; from Socrates onward many thoughtful people have held that "the really important thing is not to live, but to live well."[8]

Thus it seems that the Skinnerian is either giving us a mere causal account of why people in fact accept certain values, or at best a procedure for determining the relative value of alternative procedures and institutions, granted some more ultimate criteria of value are presupposed. This is typical of such attempts at scientific ethics, which generally attempt to determine values on the basis of what "works," without recognizing that one cannot evaluate the consequences of actions without already agreeing on some conception of "success."

political theory and the loss of the personal
Every normative political theory is ultimately rooted in a philosophical vision of human nature. This is as true of a nineteenth-century thinker like Marx as it was for Plato and his *Republic*.

Indeed, with the discovery of Marx's early manuscripts, with their arresting vision of man's potential as an active agent, combined with the analysis of the loss of that potential through "alienation," a much more profound understanding of Marxism is now possible.

Reflection on the close relationship between a philosophic conception of man and political theory raises the troubling question as to the implications of the rejection of the image of the personal for yet another area. Those who hold dear the democratic conception of society may well find that democratic ideals cohere badly with the mechanistic conception of human beings.

The premise which lies behind liberal democracy seems to be that the individual has a right to participate in those decisions which affect him. "No taxation without representation." No particular group or class has a monopoly on social wisdom and virtue. Though not every interest can be satisfied, society is served best if all interests have a right to be articulated and represented, and if appropriate mechanisms are devised whereby, after the free exchange of ideas and arguments, the interests of the majority can be satisfied while providing some protection for minority interests as well. All of this appears to presuppose that individuals are capable of making reasonable judgments about what is in their own best interests and the interests of society as a whole, or at least that their ability to make such judgments is no worse than the ability of some special person or class.

Many individuals have been frightened by the totalitarian possibilities in human engineering. Recent developments make it increasingly apparent that Orwell's *1984* was frighteningly realistic in many respects. The point which I wish to make is that the behavioral sciences do not merely constitute a neutral technology which could be employed for purposes of totalitarian control. Insofar as these sciences are regarded as undermining the image of the personal, they provide more than practical possibilities for controlling human behavior; they constitute a theoretical justification for rejecting the ideal of democracy in favor of rule by a knowledgeable elite.

This is a *theoretical* point. I am not claiming that behavioral scientists are as a class more power hungry than other men, or more prone to authoritarian ideologies. The claim is that a certain conception about the nature of man seems to fit authoritarian models of government better than it does democratic models. If human beings are seen, not as responsible agents, but as determined products of certain conditions, whether those conditions be regarded as biological or socio-economic, then the concept of political activity as a decision-making process seems absurd. Political persuasion becomes political propaganda. Rather than seeking to inform individuals about the issues and their interests so as to facilitate responsible decision-making, one seeks to manipulate public opinion so as to produce the desired outcome. What is genuinely disturbing is the extent to which this manipulative model is already accepted as the norm in American politics.

When society is viewed, not as a community of conscious agents who attempt to satisfy conflicting and partly shared interests through discussion and joint action but as a mechanism whose behavior can be described in terms of laws, democracy is undermined. The proper attitude towards such a mechanism would seem to be that of the engineer who understands those laws and can manipulate certain factors to achieve certain outcomes.

The frightening thing about Skinner's *Beyond Freedom and Dignity* is not his brash claims about the future effectiveness of a technology of control. These claims have not been verified. Rather it is the rationale which he provides for forthrightly applying such a technology. "You are already conditioned; you are already part of the machine," Skinner seems to claim. You must not object to control because you are already completely controlled. The issue is whether we will continue to limp along with the old, irrational controls or whether we will consciously subject society to the rational system of controls to be devised by the behavioral scientist.

The question Skinner needs to answer is "Who will exercise this control?" Skinner himself seems not to be terribly worried about this question. As a consistent mechanist, he understands it to be a problem in social engineering, not a problem which concerns the character or values of the controller. What is needed is a society in which those who are controlled exercise "counter-control" on their controllers.

The relation between the controller and the controlled is reciprocal.

The scientist in the laboratory, studying the behavior of a pigeon, designs contingencies and observes their effects. His apparatus exerts a conspicuous control on the pigeon, but we must not overlook the control exerted by the pigeon. The behavior of the pigeon has determined the design of the apparatus and the procedures in which it is used.[9]

One might suppose that the controlled citizens of an engineered society would likewise determine the "design of the apparatus and the procedures in which it is used." Proponents of democracy will hardly find this comforting. Skinner assures us that "the ultimate strength of a controller depends upon the strength of those whom he controls"[10] and that "under present conditions of competition it is unlikely that a government can survive which does not govern in the best interests of everyone."[11]

This last quote reads like a curious hangover from personalistic talk. What a consistent Skinner should have said is that no government is likely to survive which does not attempt to accomplish *its ends* by paying respect to the laws which describe the behavior of the mechanism. The question of what ends are to be pursued (what is in the best interests of individuals) is still to be answered by the scientific expert. If Skinner is right, the experts' values will themselves be a product of conditioning. But that in no way guarantees that those values will be humane. The "counter-control" does *not* guarantee that the government will act for the best interests of the governed. If Skinner's contention that it is always in the best interest of controllers to act with the interests of the controlled in mind is correct, then democracy seems unnecessary. A totalitarian dictator or racial oligarchy should be just as concerned for the best interests of everyone as a government freely elected by and responsible to the people. But in reality the facts are otherwise.

Even if we accepted Skinner's vision of an engineered society, the controllers would still face the first two problems which this chapter outlined.[12] If they no longer saw themselves as persons but as products of a mechanism, could the controllers continue to have faith in their own integrity as men of science? And could they themselves continue to believe in the values which they see themselves as conditioned to hold? To what ends shall their power be exercised?

7

grappling with the loss

Personalism seems to be in trouble, but we are in trouble if personalism is not viable. This is the conclusion we have reached after an initial look at the problem, a brief analysis of the view of man which emerges from certain contemporary sciences and an analysis of the implications of abandoning the image of the personal, particularly for morality and epistemology.

contradiction or resolution?

Is it possible to reconcile the image of the personal with the image of man which emerges from the contemporary behavioral sciences? Could the conflict between the two be merely apparent? To the Christian thinker, it is an article of faith that truth is ultimately unified, since "all truth is God's truth." To the extent that the scientific image and the image of the personal are both true, they must, therefore, be capable of being reconciled in some way.

Such an article of faith, of course, hardly resolves the problem. For one thing it leaves open the question as to how much truth each "image" possesses. For the Christian "all truth is God's truth" is a platitude. Like all platitudes it has value. It means that the Christian does not have to fear truth. Whatever its apparent source, truth is from God. But again, like all platitudes, this one does not resolve particular problems. The Christian must still decide what is true, and he is still faced with a difficult problem when apparent truths drawn from science seem to conflict with other apparent truths presupposed by Scripture and ordinary experience.

In the first chapter, we noted two sources of the problem: scientism and a particular philosophy of science. Scientism is the thesis that all truth is derivable by scientific method; the truth which science gives us is both *ultimate* and *complete*. There are no areas of reality which science cannot investigate, and science gives us the final truth about the nature of that reality. Personalism finds itself in trouble when scientism is wedded to a particular philosophy of science. This view of science we shall designate the "unity of science thesis." This thesis is really two-fold: it consists not merely in the assertion that there is one method which is proper to all the sciences, but in the conviction that this method is the one provided by the natural sciences understood in a particular way. On this view, science is characterized by the search for causal laws of a mechanical type, laws which are empirically verified or falsified on the basis of the predictions they make possible. This is the ideal embodied in Comte's "law of three stages," and we discovered it to be the crucial element in the development of the various sciences which have dispensed with personalistic explanations of human actions.

six routes to resolution

We can now characterize some possible responses to the problem of the person. Three fundamental types emerge, each of which comes in two forms. The first type we shall designate the *Reinterpreter* because it consists in conceding the truth of the scientific view of man and attempting to reinterpret the image of the personal in order to make it consistent with the scientific view. Within this view we can usefully distinguish those who believe that the personalistic view is genuinely false and hence needs to be radically reinterpreted (or really modified) from those who believe that the personalistic view, properly understood, is compatible with the scientific view and requires no radical changes but only proper understanding. The former type of Reinterpreter we shall call a *Capitulator,* the latter a *Compatibilist.*

The second type of response to the problem is the position taken by the *Limiters of Science*. They find scientism to be the villain of the piece. On this view, the image of the personal does not conflict with genuine science when we have a proper understanding of the nature and limits of science. There are two ways to draw these limits. Some deny the completeness of science. They understand the boundaries of science to be territorial in nature. Certain areas of reality are immune or off limits to the scientific investigator. We shall call this type of thinker a *Territorialist*. A second type of Limiter holds that science is limited by perspective. Although there are no limits to the sorts of things scientists may study, looking at reality from a scientific perspective inevitably colors one's view and makes it impossible to perceive certain dimensions of what is viewed. This type of critic we shall term a *Perspectivalist*.

The third type of response we shall consider centers its critical fire on the philosophy of science which underlies the behavioral sciences. Those who hold this view attack the "unity of science thesis." We shall call them *Humanizers of Science*. We can again distinguish two types, depending on whether the object of criticism is the particular conception of scientific method we have discussed or the thesis that there is only one scientific method. Those who oppose the positivist view of science as a whole we shall label *Generalists*, since they emphasize what they consider to be the humanization of science in general. Those who object to the idea of *one* scientific method, but admit that the positivist view of science may be applicable to some sciences we shall term *Particularists*, since they are primarily interested in humanizing the particular sciences that deal with man, opposing what they see as a methodological imperialism on the part of those who see the natural sciences as paradigms for all sciences.

To summarize—those grappling with the problem can center their critical fire on three possible areas: (1) the image of the personal itself, (2) scientism or (3) the "unity of science thesis." Reinterpreters scrutinize (1); they concede the truth of the scientific view and attempt to modify the personalistic view so as to adapt to it. Limiters of Science attack (2); they attempt to preserve the image of the personal by discerning the limits of scientific knowledge. Humanizers of Science look most closely at (3); they attempt to preserve the image of the personal by internal reforms of science.

Another way of delineating these responses is to analyze their reactions to the following four propositions:

SCIENTISM:

1a. Science gives us truth about the *whole* of reality.

1b. Science gives us the *ultimate* truth about those realities it deals with.

UNITY OF SCIENCE THESIS:

2a. There is one method which all genuine sciences employ.

2b. This method consists of giving deterministic causal explanations which are empirically testable.

Reinterpreters accept all four of these propositions. Compatibilists believe that, properly understood, the image of the personal is compatible with their implications. Capitulators believe that the image of the personal is not compatible with these implications and must be radically modified. On their view, we must change our concept of what it is to be a person. The Compatibilist merely thinks we must gain a better understanding of our current view of the person.

Limiters of Science reject either 1a or 1b, which together constitute *scientism*. Territorialists reject proposition 1a, claiming that there are some sorts of realities which cannot be investigated scientifically. Perspectivalists reject 1b, claiming that though science may give us some truth about everything, it may not give us the ultimate truth about anything.

Humanizers of Science reject either 2a or 2b. Particularists admit that the positivist view of science is appropriate in some cases but not in the case of the sciences that deal with man. Hence they deny 2a—the thesis that there is *one* proper scientific method. Generalists deny 2b and question whether even the natural sciences are adequately characterized in this way. These six views are summarized in the following chart:

REINTERPRETERS (accept both "scientism" and the "unity of science thesis")

    Compatibilists (properly interpreted, the image of the personal is compatible with mechanism)

    Capitulators (nothing essential is lost by modifying the

image of the personal to make it compatible with mechanism)
LIMITERS OF SCIENCE (reject "scientism")
   Territorialists (reject 1a)
   Perspectivalists (reject 1b)
HUMANIZERS OF SCIENCE (reject "unity of science thesis")
   Particularists (reject 2a)
   Generalists (reject 2b)

ideal types

These six ways of dealing with the crisis of the person are best conceived as "ideal types," to use a term popularized by sociologist Max Weber. They are not necessarily mutually exclusive. Actual thinkers may combine one or more of these approaches. In fact, it would be unusual to find an absolutely pure representative of any of them. Nevertheless, despite their ideal character, I believe they are more than mere logical possibilities. Recognizable aspects of these responses can be identified among many thoughtful people, including scientists themselves.

If the question is raised as to which of these positions is *the* Christian response to the problem, the correct response is "all and none." All of these positions represent possible bases for a reasonable, coherent Christian response to the sciences of man. None of them is exclusively Christian in the sense that identical or very similar views could not be held by a non-Christian. For this reason, I believe that these reflections, though written from a Christian perspective, will also be of interest to non-Christian humanists.

My own biases will probably be only too evident as we proceed. And I shall not hide my convictions as to what seems to be a promising approach. Before coming to my own conclusions, however, I believe that it will be helpful to attempt a fair and objective review of all the options available, highlighting what seem to me to be the strengths and weaknesses of each. This will not only help the reader to understand my own conclusions; hopefully it will assist him in thinking through the problem for himself. If he should find my own thinking disagreeable, he may at least have been helped to understand the strengths and weaknesses of his own view better.

8 reinterpreters of the personal

Reinterpretation: this option immediately confronts the Christian thinker struggling with the problem of the person in a mechanistic universe. Basically the Reinterpreter accepts the four propositions by which we defined the unity of science thesis and the view we called scientism (See page 90 above). Hence, this type of response does not question the legitimacy and truth of the general scientific picture of man, though he may of course question the validity of particular scientific hypotheses.

Having conceded the validity of the scientific perspective, the Reinterpreter then attempts to argue that this perspective does not really threaten what a humanist thinker—Christian or non-Christian—ought to say about the person. He will perhaps argue that the traditional personalistic view has been misunderstood and that, properly interpreted, it is compatible with what the scientist tells us. This type of Reinterpreter is a Compatibilist. Or he will concede that the traditional view of the person is incompatible with the scientific picture and must be radically modified or even scrapped. This second type of Reinterpreter demands that we change our concept of "personhood." What he must claim is that nothing essentially true is lost by this change. This second type of Reinterpreter is a Capitulator.

The great strength of a Reinterpreter position is that it does not involve the personalistic thinker in any conflict with science. The Christian Reinterpreter is attempting to learn from the mistakes Christians have made in the past. Everyone is familiar with the notorious attempts on the part of the church to stifle the theories of Copernicus and Galileo because of their alleged incompatibility with Scripture and "the Christian world view." Time after time, it seems, Christians have opposed new scientific theories because they have unwittingly misunderstood the essential content of their faith. Eventually, the new scientific theory is accepted and it is later seen that the conflict was misguided, based on a misinterpretation of the Christian message. The Reinterpreter does not wish to repeat this pattern and find himself accused of being an obscurantist who blocks scientific inquiry and finds himself on the wrong side of history.

Basically, the position of a Reinterpreter is that the universe is indeed mechanistic and that there is no reason to think that human behavior is any exception. The idea that there are "gaps" in the scientific chain of causes in which "spiritual" or "mental" reality might reside is a weak foundation for a Christian understanding of man. No, the Reinterpreter says, let there be no weak, defensive, holding actions, in which a person-of-the-gaps is gradually enfeebled and diminished. It is true that scientific explanation of human behavior, whether concerned with physiological, psychological or socio-cultural mechanisms, is as yet far from complete, but this ignorance is merely a sign of the complexity of the subject and finiteness of the scientists; it is sure to diminish in time.

In what sense can such a view be Christian? The point of integration here is the creative sovereignty of God. Proponents of such a view stress the biblical concept of God as the one who continuously maintains in being every aspect of the created order. There is no biblical warrant, they assert, for the view that God determines the outcome of some events, while leaving others undetermined. Man himself, the Reinterpreter says, is seen in Scripture as "dust," part of the created order. Hence there is no biblical warrant for thinking him to be the great exception to the laws of the created order.

Here the critic will ask, "But what of the biblical picture of man as a free and responsible agent? What happens to freedom and responsibility in such a mechanistic framework?" On these questions the Compatibilist and Capitulator will diverge. The Compatibilist will attempt to argue that freedom and responsibility, properly understood, are consistent with this deterministic framework. The Capitulator will argue that the concepts of freedom and responsibility, as these terms are generally understood, simply do not apply to human beings and are not essential features of a Christian view of the person. Let us discuss each of these two "subspecies" in more detail.

capitulators

The really consistent Capitulator is, I believe, a rarity. This is a position for which I do not have a great deal of sympathy, as is perhaps evidenced by the prejudicial name I have assigned it.

Among non-Christian humanists, this position is perhaps more common. For example, an acceptance of determinism and the repudiation of the thesis that individuals are responsible for their actions is frequently claimed to be a humane view of the person. Such a view would not only outlaw the barbaric practice of "punishment;"[1] it would also lead to a great decrease in human strife and unhappiness. Imagine a world where individuals and nations no longer wrangled over who is to be held "at fault" for various troubles, a world lacking the charges and counter-charges of our own. This type of Capitulator may argue that a fatalistic perspective on life is capable of giving humans a sense of peace and serenity as they go about their daily tasks.[2] Far from degrading the person, an understanding of the necessity of events is the source of man's true dignity.

A Christian Capitulator will certainly stress the biblical concept of the sovereignty of God. He will claim that nowhere does the Bible clearly teach any philosophical doctrine of "free will." Rather the Bible pictures a God who controls and determines all things for his own purposes. Although the Calvinist in some ways is more likely to be a Compatibilist, the Capitulator has every right to appeal to certain themes in Calvinistic theology (and its basis in Scripture) to justify his position. That is, although not all Calvinists would be happy with Capitulationism (or with any form of mechanism), it seems likely that the Capitulator might be happy with Calvinism (or at least his reading of Calvin).

After all, Calvin himself speaks of "the eternal decree of God, by which he determined with himself whatever he wished to happen with regard to every man."[3] Calvin explicitly denies that God's decree that some will be saved and others perish is based on God's foreknowledge of human choices; he claims that God's acts are based solely on his own purposes.[4] Calvin denies that any meaningful distinction can be drawn between the will and the permission of God.[5] God does not leave some human acts undetermined. He does not merely allow human beings to choose eternal life or eternal damnation. They choose as they were predestined to choose.

The mechanical laws which the scientist discovers are simply interpreted by the Capitulator as the *means* whereby God's sovereign decrees are accomplished. The fact that these laws may be deterministic and the fact that they entail that the ultimate causes of human behavior lie outside the agent himself does not trouble the Capitulator, who regards these causes, whether environmental or hereditary, as part of God's creative ordering of events.

When the question is raised as to whether God is justified in holding individuals responsible for acts which, in a sense, were ultimately determined by God himself, the Capitulator steadfastly denies the legitimacy of the question. What right do human beings have to question the justice of God or to inquire as to the reasons for his choices?

You will say to me then, "Why does he still find fault? For who can resist his will?" But, who are you, a man, to answer back to God? Will what is molded say to its molder, "Why have you made me thus?" Has the potter no right over the clay, to make out of the same lump one vessel for beauty and another for menial use? (Romans 9: 19-21 RSV).

The Apostle Paul claims here that men simply have no standing before God, no right to an accounting. God, as sovereign Creator, is entitled to create diverse types of entities and then treat them as the kind of entity they are. "Vessels of wrath" are fitted for destruction; "vessels of mercy" are "prepared beforehand for glory," to "make known the riches of his glory" (Rom. 9:22-23).

Of course the Capitulator can also be challenged to explain other themes found in Scripture. Only a little later than the passage just quoted, Paul exclaims:

The scripture says, "No one who believes in him will be put to shame." . . . For, "every one who calls upon the name of the Lord will be saved." (Romans 10:11 and 13)

The whole of Scripture is full of exhortations from God and God's messengers to choose rightly and to refrain from evil. Such exhortations hardly make sense in a context where human beings do not have any freedom to make decisions. If all human beings inevitably do the will of God, then what sense can be made of a God who pleads with his people to turn from sin to himself? And would not such a view make God the author of sin? It seems difficult to avoid this charge if human beings are not conceded at least relative autonomy in their acts and decisions.

compatibilists

It is because of these problems that most Reinterpreters find the Compatibilist position more attractive than the hard-nosed Capitulator's view. The Compatibilist believes that he can, in a sense, have his cake and eat it too. He claims the traditional view of the person as free and responsible is, properly understood, compatible with what the Capitulator asserts about mechanisms and divine sovereignty.

The assertion that "man is both free and determined" may mean several things. It may amount to intellectual double talk, a dishonest attempt to have it both ways. That is, it may simply be equivalent to asserting that A and not-A are both true. Called to question on his determinism, this type of Compatibilist willingly admits that freedom is *also* true, but fails to give any account of *how* the two are compatible, although a sense of paradox is plainly present.

This sort of position is rescued from dishonesty if the individual who asserts that both freedom and determinism are true forthrightly acknowledges the limitations of the human intellect in dealing with such a question. Perhaps the contradiction is only apparent, the result of our inability to clearly conceive of the two

97

concepts. After all, why should the whole of reality be intelligible to our feeble human reason? The whole business is an admitted paradox, a mystery or enigma, but it is one which we cannot escape affirming.

This sort of intellectual modesty is in my view a perfectly legitimate stance, provided that it is the outcome of honest intellectual struggle, rather than an evasion of it. But it seems to me that the Compatibilist who takes this line is really on the way towards becoming a Limiter of Science of some sort. For he is asserting that there are some kinds of truths or aspects of reality which are not intelligible to the human intellect and thus not amenable to scientific inquiry.

The most consistent and sophisticated way of defending Compatibilism and reconciling determinism and freedom is based on a careful analysis of the concepts of freedom and responsibility. Why must we assume that freedom and causal determinism are incompatible? Do we mean by a free event merely one that is random or uncaused? Is our ability to predict a person's behavior inconsistent with our holding him responsible for what he does? The answer to both questions seems to this sort of Compatibilist to be negative.

On his view, freedom and determinism are not really opposites at all. The opposite of freedom is coercion or compulsion; the opposite of determinism is randomness or chance. But freedom is not identical with randomness and causal determination is not the same as coercion or compulsion by some external force.

A free act, one for which a person is to be held responsible, is simply one which is caused by the character or will of the person in question. When someone holds a gun to my ribs and asks for my money, my response is hardly free. But in many cases I am under no such compulsion. The causes of my behavior lie within my own psyche, or personality, or brain. I am responsible for such acts since I originate them. Though God may ultimately determine the outcome since he maintains and controls the whole created order, nevertheless within that created order persons exist and their choices and decisions are part of the means or "secondary causes" whereby God accomplishes his ends.

The critic may here interpose that freedom requires that the person "could have chosen differently." Our reconciler of freedom and determinism replies that a person who has acted freely *could* have chosen differently. That is, he could have chosen differently *if* he wished to, *if* his character had been different, *if* his genes had been different and so forth. Thus the thesis that "he could have chosen otherwise" is interpreted in such a way that it is compatible with the thesis: "Given the chain of causes, his choice is determined."

This sort of Compatibilism seems to be the type which Calvinist theologians have found most congenial. For example, the Westminster Confession states that, "although in relation to the foreknowledge and decree of God, the first cause, all things come to pass immutably and infallibly, yet by the same providence he ordereth them to fall out, according to the nature of second causes, either necessarily, freely, or contingently."[6] According to the Westminster Divines, a strong belief in predestination was compatible with the thesis that "God hath endued the will of man with that natural liberty, that is neither forced nor by any absolute necessity of nature determined to good or evil."[7]

When developed along these lines, the Compatibilist position is powerful and attractive, and it provides a coherent framework for a Christian who wishes to integrate his faith and the findings of the social sciences. Nevertheless, there are some hard questions that must be asked of it, primarily concerning the analyses of freedom and responsibility which have been offered. In this deterministic framework, is the operative concept of responsibility really that necessary for moral responsibility? In this framework are people not responsible for their acts in precisely the same sense in which machines (computers?) are responsible for their "behavior," or in which an apple tree is responsible for producing its fruit? Doesn't the notion of moral freedom demand not merely that the person could have done otherwise *if* some things had been different (his genes, his background, his character), but that the person has at least some alternatives among which he may choose, even if nothing about the causal nexus prior to that point of decision had been different? When we hold a person morally responsible do we not say to him, "You could have done otherwise *even given* your past and present." When we ourselves deliberate about an act, do we not necessarily presuppose that the alternatives we consider are genuine alternatives?

When all is said and done, it must be asked whether the Compatibilist position differs in any significant way from the Capitulator's view, except verbally. The Compatibilist asserts that in the case of some acts, persons act freely in the sense that, *if* certain things in their past had been different, nothing would have prevented them from making an alternative choice. The person is free to choose as he wills, or as he desires, or in accordance with his character. However, what he wills, what he desires, or the make-up of his character is in fact determined. Given the chain of causes, his act follows inevitably. And that chain of causes is, according to the mechanist, determined in turn. In what sense then are these possibilities *real*? It seems that the freedom offered by the Compatibilist is purely hypothetical, dependent upon conditions which not only are not but could not be realized. If this is so, then it would seem that the Compatibilist is faced with the same difficulties as the Capitulator.

For these reasons I do not myself regard the Reinterpreter view as a promising option for either the Christian or non-Christian humanist. But it continues to be supported by many careful thinkers and is therefore worthy of respect as well as continued critical examination. However, there is one sense in which a Christian cannot be a "pure" Reinterpreter as we have defined the position. A Reinterpreter is someone who accepts the two propositions of scientism: scientific truth is both ultimate and complete. The Christian Reinterpreter can only acknowledge a relative completeness and finality to the scientific account. From the perspective of science, the mechanistic account may be final and complete. And the Reinterpreter attempts to make his view of man consistent with this scientific picture. He will, nevertheless, if he is truly Christian, insist that the scientific story is not the whole story. Science gives us an account of the *how* of God's doings, the means whereby God's decrees are accomplished. But science cannot tell us the *why*; God's purposes in ordering the universe as he does are opaque to the scientist. The meaning of an act is not exhausted by the mechanical account.[8] Hence the Christian Reinterpreter is always on the verge of becoming a Limiter of Science, and it is to that perspective I now turn.

9

limiters of science

Limiters of Science believe that the conflict between the image of the personal and the scientific picture of man is generated by scientism. The origin of the problem, they say, lies in a failure to reflect realistically and critically on the nature and limits of science and the scientific method. They thus deny one or both of the propositions by which we defined scientism; science on their view is either incomplete or non-ultimate. Either there are some areas of reality which science cannot investigate, or there are dimensions to the reality which science does investigate which science cannot perceive. Those who proclaim some areas to be off-limits are Territorialists. Those who think of the limits as limits of perspective are Perspectivalists.

It is important to understand that the validity of scientism is not itself a scientific issue. The assertion that science gives us the whole truth and the ultimate truth about reality is a philosophical claim not a scientific assertion. It is not a scientific hypothesis, but a hypothesis about science. Therefore the Limiter of Science is not necessarily antiscientific. He is not challenging the validity of scientific inquiry, but asking us to reflect on the value and limits of scientific inquiry.

In fact, for the most part the conception of science held by the

Limiter of Science is congenial to the hard-nosed scientist. The Limiter of Science grants the unity of science thesis. He does not, as does the Humanizer of Science, attack the conception that there is one fundamental scientific method. Nor does he challenge the thesis that this method consists in the search for general laws of a mechanical nature, laws which are verified by objective empirical observations. His quarrel is not with science itself but scientism.

territorialists

Territorialists conceive the limits of science in terms of regions of reality—types of entities that science is incapable of dealing with. They therefore deny proposition 1a: "Science gives us the truth about the whole of reality."

The classic example of Territorialism is Descartes' mind-body dualism, which we discussed briefly in Chapter 2. Descartes made his peace with mechanistic science and human freedom by a dualistic ontology. Reality is composed of two radically different sorts of stuff, *res extensa* and *res cogitans*. In the material realm mechanistic explanations are complete. But the human mind, Descartes said, was not a material thing but a spiritual reality, attached to a body but occupying no specific spatial location. The contents of the mind were said to be essentially private, available only to introspection and beyond the reach of a science which can only deal with publicly observable, spatial entities. This dualistic perspective could fairly have been called the "establishment view" prior to the twentieth century. Even today it seems to dominate the thought-patterns and speech of ordinary life. The tendency to think of persons as possessing a nonmaterial soul is widespread.

Other types of dualism than mind-body dualism are also conceivable. Territorial tendencies are present in the conceptions of the dual realms of nature and spirit found among some neo-Kantian and idealist philosophers. On this view, nature is the realm of necessity where events are governed by universal laws. The world of the spirit, however, is the world of freedom—the realm of the unique event which resists law-like explanation. This is only one strain in idealist thought. In some ways those thinkers are more like Perspectivalists; in some ways more like Humanizers of Science. Hence we shall treat them more fully later on.

Since the advent of mechanistic science, mind-body dualism has been dominant in orthodox Protestant thought. Many Protestant theologians have followed Descartes in seeing man as body *plus* soul, or body *plus* spirit (or soul *and* spirit). The biblical bases of such a view are well-known, although it is controversial to what extent such dualistic views are Hebraic or Greek in origin. Paul speaks of the body as a tent which we live in, or a suit of clothes (2 Cor. 5:1-4). He also says that to be absent from the body is to be present with the Lord (2 Cor. 5:6-8), implying that personal existence may continue apart from the body. Christ says we are not to fear those who can kill the body, but he who can destroy *both* body and soul (Mt. 10:28). Implicit in the whole biblical account is a conception of man as *more* than just dust, and this truth is frequently expressed by calling this something more a soul or spirit. (In some cases soul and spirit are distinguished and both are ascribed to human beings.) One obvious advantage of dualism from a Christian perspective is that it makes sense of the Christian teaching that physical death is not the final end of personal existence. If the person is identified with the body (or made completely dependent on the body as in epiphenomenalism), it is hard to explain why the cessation of the body's function is not the end of that person.

When applied to the social sciences, dualistic views hold some rather militant implications. Though perhaps reticent to do so because of the prestige of science, a consistent dualist, it would seem, ought to charge naturalistically inclined social scientists with trespassing on a forbidden domain. While physiology as a science of the human *body* may seem legitimate, the notion of a science of man which ignores the soul (that intellectual valuing center of activity which represents the real person or at least the center of the real person) is a flagrant contradiction in terms. The success of the sciences which have dispensed with a nonphysical soul might be regarded as circular. Having begun from a perspective which essentially defines spiritual reality out of existence, the social scientist completes his circle of explanation by announcing that nowhere in his investigation did he discover such a reality or feel the need to postulate it. For example, the fact that brain physiologists have so far discovered no need to postulate any but mechanical causes in their explanations can be understood as a consequence of their presuppositions. Brain scientists committed to the scientific method look only for mechanistic causes; hence they will hardly find any other kind. And the dualist will point out that our present knowledge of how the brain functions is so limited that it hardly justifies the boundless faith in a mechanistic account which some seem to have. Indeed several distinguished brain scientists continue to regard dualism as plausible.[1] The dualist has no quarrel with mechanistic science as long as it is aware of its limits, but he is implicitly a militant critic of any scientific account of the person which purports to be the complete truth. And on his view, no one who ignores conscious processes can hope to give a rational account of human behavior.

Territorialism, however, is not without its own problems. Chief among these is putting Humpty Dumpty together again after he has been fragmented. That is, having sundered the man from his body, or culture from nature, the dualistic thinker has great difficulty in understanding the evidently intimate relationships between his discrete regions. Mind-body dualists have traditionally seen the relationship of mind to body and vice versa as one of causal interaction. Causal interaction, however, does not seem adequate to account for the peculiarly intimate relationship which I have to my body. A threat to my body is a threat to *me*. The multitude of intimate relationships between physiological and mental happenings discovered by modern brain research, while perhaps compatible with dualism, do not seem congenial to it.

A second problem with dualism lies in its evidential base. Since the position of the Territorialist is that empirical science cannot really investigate the mind, he cannot offer scientific support for his contentions. His main appeals are to our immediate intuitive awareness of the mental and to a variety of philosophical arguments designed to show the radically nonphysical character of the mind.

For example, dualists often claim that consciousness must be distinct from the body because the body (including the brain) as a physical object is in principle publicly observable. The mind, on the other hand, is claimed to be private, observable only to the individual person. Thus the two cannot be identified, and the mind-brain identity theory must be false. Against the behaviorist, the dualist points out that the individual often knows his own mental states directly; he does not merely *infer* that he is in pain by observing his behavior. Against the epiphenomenalist, the interactionist dualist points out the obvious causal role ideas and other mental events have played in history, both world history and the history of the individual.[2]

Although these arguments have been criticized by nondualists, they remain formidable. To criticize them in detail would take us into philosophical issues of great technicality and complexity.[3] Nevertheless they do not seem as invincible as they once did. The *Zeitgeist* has definitely been against the dualist. To many, including many philosophers, dualism just does not seem a live option today. A philosopher who seeks to ignore such cultural biases will hardly find that to be a reason to give up dualism. Nevertheless, even philosophers must inevitably find some options more promising and worthy of an investment of critical energy than others. Philosophies are partially, if not completely, philosophies of their age.

The biblical basis of dualism has also been challenged by many thinkers today, including some evangelicals.[4] The Bible does not always use dualistic language and it is arguable that the central teaching of Scripture is towards the unity of the person.[5] Perhaps the dualistic language of Scripture is intended as the "language of appearance," as is the case where the Bible speaks of the sun rising and setting. Nevertheless, the claims of dualism, both philosophical and theological, have by no means been disposed of, and it remains a possible perspective from which to critically analyze the sciences of man.

perspectivalists

Our second type of Limiter of Science is the thinker who denies the ultimacy of science. He sees the limits of science as limits of outlook or perspective. He does not deny that science can legitimately treat any and every region of reality. However, though the scientist may have something to say about everything, he does not tell the whole story about some things (perhaps not anything).

The scientific method is a commitment to a certain way of seeing things, which enables one to see some important things which would otherwise be missed. But it is not the only possible perspective; to gain a view of man as he really is—to gain metaphysical truth—one must not look only to science.

In contrast to the dualist, the Perspectivalist may stress the unity of man. He may admit that to some extent it is true to say that a man is his body, or that he is a complex of socio-cultural relationships. However, the Perspectivalist stresses that this unitary reality can be seen from different viewpoints, and, when seen from these multiple viewpoints, different aspects appear. Science is limited not by what sorts of objects can be studied, but by what can be said about the objects it studies.

Perspectivalism of course plays heavily on the metaphor of vision in which we accept the possibility of a plurality of different descriptions of an object; these reflect differences in the viewers' interests, skills and viewpoint. Unfortunately, it is difficult to go very much beyond this metaphor, which some do not find particularly clear or helpful. The root idea seems to be that observing, describing and explaining are activities which presuppose a larger context. One does not simply observe and explain; one observes and explains in a particular way, on a particular occasion, for particular purposes. For different purposes different sorts of observations and explanations are appropriate. These differences might show up in the fact that a particular mode of observation and explanation must employ a restricted vocabulary, with other modes employing other vocabularies. But the assumption which seems to me to underlie this "linguistic" account of Perspectivalism is that reality itself, which lends itself to these various vocabularies, has a richness and complexity which transcends particular human descriptions of it.

In relationship to the biblical conception of man, the Perspectivalist is likely to stress the different functions and purposes of the biblical and scientific accounts. The Bible is not a scientific textbook; it tells us who did it and why rather than what and how. As man is a part of the created order, it is no cause for alarm that scientists have begun to describe man and explain his behavior as part of that order. Such scientific accounts have their value, but they cannot replace (because they do not compete with) accounts which view man as a moral agent made in the image of God.

One excellent example of a Perspectivalist is the French Catholic, Gabriel Marcel.[6] While emphasizing the unity of the person and the body, Marcel nonetheless argues that scientific accounts necessarily perceive the person as part of an objective order, a set of problems to be solved. Concrete or lived-experience of the person, however, is of an entirely different order. In such experience, the person is seen as a *presence* not as object, and the difficulties encountered are mysteries to be explored, rather than problems to be solved. Marcel believes that the "mind-body problem" is not a problem but a mystery. My relationship to my body is too intimate to allow me to objectify it as a thing and then ask, "How am I related to this thing called my body?" My body is too intimately bound up with my identity to regard it as an object to possess or a tool to be used. However, reductionist materialisms are equally wrong in trying to reduce the person to a mechanical object. The truth is, according to Marcel, that I experience my own body not primarily as an object but as the expression or embodiment of my conscious purposes. Consciousness is incarnated, and, if the body is the incarnation of consciousness, it cannot be merely a mechanical object. To support this mystery/problem distinction Marcel gives a critique of scientific method, attempting to show that it is grounded in an *attitude* towards the world, an attitude of mistrust which precludes perception of the fully personal, and which, if extended beyond the realm of science, results in a total dehumanization of existence.

As evidence that Marcel's view is not simply special pleading to save his Christian faith, it is worth noting that similar views are expressed by non-Christian existential philosophers, such as Maurice Merleau-Ponty and Jean-Paul Sartre. Neither of these thinkers is a dualist; both would admit that in some sense a person is his body. But they would deny that a person can view his own body simply as a mechanical thing; it is something which is "on the side of the subject."[7] Merleau-Ponty also talks of the mind as incarnated and speaks of the body as "our point of view on the world, the place where the spirit takes on a certain physical and historical situation."[8] The views of these existentialists all seem to be that though the person is a unified subject and is not to be thought of in dualistic terms, that unity is a unity with complex, rich dimensions which are lost or distorted when the person is viewed purely as an object for scientific study. In many ways, however, philosophers such as Merleau-Ponty are closer to the Humanizer of Science position, and we shall therefore discuss the movement known as phenomonology in Chapter 10.

Surprisingly enough, although they express their insights in a radically different manner, many British and American philosophers express views on the person today which seem remarkably close to these existentialists. These philosophers are generally referred to as conceptual analysts, and many of them were influenced by the curious figure of Ludwig Wittgenstein.[9] In the last twenty-five years these thinkers have developed what might be called the philosophy of action. By analyzing the concept of an action, as well as such related concepts as "reason," "intention," "willing," "desiring," these thinkers have attempted to show the impossibility of reducing descriptions and explanations of actions to descriptions and explanations of what we have termed mere events. Understanding an action requires seeing it from a first-person perspective. When understood from this first-person perspective (the perspective of the agent), decisions must be regarded, not as future facts to be predicted on the basis of empirical, factual evidence, but choices to be made on the basis of value-considerations. These philosophers, while not denying the possibility of a mechanistic, physiological science which deals with human behavior, assert that there are aspects of human behavior which such a science would inevitably miss.

two perspectivalists: jeeves and mackay

Evangelical Christian writers find Perspectivalism congenial too. There are many Perspectivalist themes in the writings of D. M. MacKay, a British brain researcher and computer scientist, though there are some elements in MacKay's thought which tend towards a Reinterpreter view. For example, in a lecture delivered at Wheaton College in July, 1975, MacKay stressed the thesis that God does not determine the outcome of some events while leaving others undetermined.[10] And in his published work, MacKay discusses the possibility that in principle a super-scientist who knew all about our brain cells could successfully predict the outcome of decisions we have not yet made, so long as he did not inform us of his prediction. Although MacKay does not claim that this will ever be possible, he does say that if it does happen, it would pose no threat to human freedom.

However, there is also a distinct perspectival thrust to MacKay's work. MacKay uses the analogy of an "electric signboard" to illustrate his view of the limits of science.[11] An electrician giving an electrical account of the sign might describe the sign completely and speak only of light bulbs, electrical circuits and so forth. In his own terms, his explanation is complete, and what he describes is identical with the sign. Yet nowhere in his account do we have any reference to what the sign says, to its message or significance. The account given by the electrician is not flawed as an electrical account; it simply reflects the limitations which are an inherent part of his perspective. To say more, we must take another vantage point. Trying to claim that the scientific perspective on man tells us all there is to know is a reductionist fallacy which MacKay labels "nothing-buttery."[12] Clearly the limits of science are not limits of territory.

No part of the world of observable events is outside the boundary of scientific study. However little the scientist may make of some of these from his professional standpoint, he is certainly entitled to try. His conclusions, however limited in scope, may be of real help in appropriate circumstances. The limitations will show up rather in the restricted kinds of description his language allows him to make of the events he studies, and the kinds of point he will be obliged to miss (theoretically) in consequence.[13]

A secular philosopher whose view of the relationship of scientific to "everyday" explanations and accounts is very similar to MacKay's is Gilbert Ryle. In his book *Dilemmas*, Ryle uses the analogy of an accountant's report on a college to illustrate the way in which an account may "cover everything" but nonetheless fail to say what is essential.[14] To attempt to explain all human behavior in terms of the laws of physics would be an example of what Ryle would regard as a category mistake. An answer which would be appropriate for one type of question is being confusedly given as an answer to a totally different type of question. To attempt to explain the behavior of a soccer player by citing physical laws would be utterly confusing. When we say, "He kicked the ball because he was trying to score a goal," we are moving in a linguistic domain distinct from that of the physicist, not doing poorly what the physical scientist does well. Ryle's concept of distinct "categories" of questions is appealing because it makes possible complementary accounts of the same phenomenon. Malcolm Jeeves, a British psychologist, clearly seems to appeal to some such notion as this in attempting to reconcile Christianity with his discipline.

I shall argue that there is no necessary conflict between the assured results of psychological researches into religious behavior and experience, and much of what has been expressed in other ways, using categories variously described as religious, theological, or spiritual, about the same behavior and experience. I believe it is making a category error to oppose what is asserted in two distinct language domains.[15]

The key problem for the Perspectivalist, as for the Territorialist, is relating what has been sundered. It is congenial to regard the mechanistic physiological account of a piece of behavior as belonging to a different "category" than the ordinary, personalistic type of account, or describing a different "dimension" of the same reality. However, if that reality is the same reality, the question must be raised as to how these different ways of describing and explaining human behavior are related. Alternate accounts of the same phenomena inevitably raise the question as to whether or not one or more of the accounts may not be superfluous. This is why the religious believer is sometimes distressed when the psychologist explains conversion as the result of biologically grounded mechanisms or behavioral reinforcement. It is also why the believer in a political theory is distressed when the sociologist explains his adoption of that theory as a result of his socio-economic status. The religious believer thinks that the conversion is the work of God. The political believer thinks that he embraces his party because it is based on sound values and has a realistic program for implementing those values. It is hard not to see these various causal accounts as rivals, especially when one attributes the change in behavior to deterministic laws, while the other speaks of free choice.

In dealing with this problem, a variety of responses is open to the Perspectivalist. One way out of the dilemma is to embrace a pragmatic or functionalist interpretation of science. On this view scientific theories are simply instruments for prediction and control. Science does not give us any truths about the way things are. The proper question to ask about a scientific theory is not "Is it true?" but "Is it useful?" Does the theory work, in the sense of allowing us to anticipate the future course of experience? If scientific theories are simply useful fictions, then they will obviously not threaten the truth of personalistic accounts of man.

On the other extreme from this pragmatic view of science are those Perspectivalists who take a realistic interpretation of science and argue that personalistic and/or theological accounts are needed to complement the scientific account. This type of position (one asserting that scientific and personalistic accounts are both true) raises in its most acute form the problem of reconciling alternative accounts of the same phenomenon.

One way Perspectivalists have dealt with this problem is by appealing to the practice of physics in regarding seemingly incompatible models of the behavior of light as complementary. It is now well-known that physicists have found it necessary in some contexts to regard light as a wave-like phenomena and in other contexts as consisting of particles. In different contexts light seems to take on characteristics of each model. After much debate it was finally decided that both models had to be employed to give an accurate account of light. The two models were not rival but complementary aspects of the same phenomenon. In a similar way, Malcolm Jeeves has argued that the sort of account given of behavior by science must be regarded as complementing a theological account.[16] The notion of complementarity is helpful in understanding the relationship of seemingly rival scientific accounts of man as well, Jeeves claims.

Critics of Perspectivalism might well wonder whether or not the analogy with the physicists' concept of complementarity is a good one. In any case, problems remain. In the case of the physicist, it is clear that the rival accounts of light are both models, and even in this case the use of such divergent models leads us to question the nature of a model. To what extent does a model give a picture of how things really are? In the case of man, the use of such divergent models as those employed by personalism and mechanism raises similar questions. The Perspectivalist must show how these different accounts are related and why both are needed. He must explain in what context it is legitimate to apply each model. And he must not forget that these complementary models are being used to describe the same reality.

The temptation to reduce the tension between these complementary accounts by modifying or reinterpreting the image of the personal will obviously be a strong one. In that case we are back to the previous chapter and our discussion of Compatibilists. And indeed, in thinkers like MacKay tendencies in that direction are marked. Such a view would not be a pure example of one of our types, but it might of course gain strength by attempting to include the advantages of both positions. The danger is ambiguity.

For an example, let us take the position of Donald MacKay on the question of freedom. MacKay claims that even if there were a completely isomorphic relationship between mental functions and the mechanical activities of the brain, so that every change in mental state corresponded to some mechanical process in the brain, that this would not affect human freedom.[17] This is so because even though an observer might, with adequate knowledge of a person's current brain state, be able in principle to predict that person's thoughts, this prediction would be valid only if the observer did not inform the agent being observed of his prediction. If the agent were informed of the prediction, the reception of this information would constitute a change in his brain state. Since the original prediction was made on the assumption that the agent's brain was in a particular state, any alteration of that state invalidates the prediction. If the observer formulates a new prediction based on his knowledge of the new brain state, then he must keep this prediction to himself as well. If he informs the agent whose beliefs are in question, then that person's brain state will again be altered and the process can go on indefinitely. The conclusion MacKay draws is that no completely determinate specification of future states of his brain (corresponding to belief states) exists which the agent would be unconditionally correct to accept, and in error to reject, if only he knew it.[18]

This is a puzzling argument and it is difficult to know what to make of it. MacKay is saying that an action which might be infallibly predicted by an onlooker is nevertheless not inevitable for the agent. What an agent would be correct to believe about his action, an observer would be in error to believe. Conversely, what an onlooker would be correct to believe, an agent would be in error to accept.

MacKay's argument does establish that the agent is free in a certain sense of the word, however the argument is interpreted. But it seems to me that two readings of the argument can be given which employ two different senses of freedom. I believe that the first of these readings is more faithful to MacKay's intentions. And I believe that this sense of freedom is not the sense which is required for moral responsibility. This first reading is the type of view which a Compatibilist would advance. The second reading, which I believe MacKay does not intend, represents the view of an authentic Perspectivalist.

On the first interpretation, all MacKay's argument does is make the familiar point that if the person is changed, then his behavior will be changed. The Compatibilist interprets freedom as the ability to act as one chooses to act. How one chooses is determined. The person is said to be free to have chosen otherwise in the sense that *if* his wishes, wants, desires, character or beliefs had been different, he could have acted differently. It follows that when a person's character, wishes, desires or beliefs are changed, the person may act differently than he would have *if* the change had not occurred. But whether the change will occur is in fact determined, and so is the resulting behavior. MacKay's argument simply tells us that *if* a change is made in a person's brain state (by being informed of a prediction about his behavior), his behavior will be different and therefore any prediction based on the former brain state would be invalidated. From the mechanistic point of view, whether the change will be made (whether the observer will inform the onlooker) is causally determined, however, and therefore the eventual outcome is determined. This result can only be avoided by assuming that the onlooker is free (in a radical sense) to inform or not to inform the object of his study of his prediction. But that assumption will not be admitted by the determinist.

MacKay would probably respond to this by noting that his argument proceeds on the assumption that the agent will *not* find out about the prediction. Even in this case, he argues, it is still true that no specification of the agent's choice exists which the agent would be correct to accept and in error to reject, if only he knew it. But this reply does not contradict our point. For the reason no such specification of the agent's choice exists which the agent would be correct to accept is that his acceptance of any such hypothesis would falsify it. MacKay is assuming that the agent will *not* find out about the prediction; hence it follows that the agent would not be correct to believe the prediction *if only he knew it*. The agent can very well know that his action is causally determined; he simply cannot know (and hence would not be correct in believing) the particular prediction which has been made by an observer, which assumes the agent will not find out about the hypothesis.

Every "soft determinist" or Compatibilist holds that the determination of an action is hypothetical in the sense that, if certain conditions do not hold, the prediction will not hold good either. MacKay has simply chosen the interesting case of a situation where these hypothetical conditions include an ignorance concerning his predicted action on the part of the agent. This does entail that no prediction of his action exists which the agent would be correct to accept if he knew it. But I do not think it shows that, given the actual conditions which do hold (including the ignorance of the agent), that the agent has more than one choice which he could make. This first reading of MacKay's argument shows only that the agent is free in the sense that he has alternatives which he could choose *if* different conditions are presupposed.

The second way of taking MacKay's argument is to interpret it as establishing that there is no logical specification of a person's beliefs about a subject for which he has not made up his mind which any person would be correct to accept. The person's future belief really is indeterminate, since any prediction about his own belief which he might make or become aware of might change that belief. On this second interpretation, the fact that the onlooker's prediction can be falsified by the agent is taken as illustrating a crucial feature of the nature of belief. Believing is not simply a physical happening; it is an activity which includes a normative element. Anyone who is engaged in deciding what he does believe is also engaged in deciding what he ought to believe.

One implication which this has is that reflecting on the causes of my beliefs may alter those beliefs. For example, if I should discover that I held a certain belief for no good reasons but rather because I had been taking a certain drug, this would tend to undermine the belief. It would undermine the belief not merely because finding this out might make some change in my brain state (although it might) but first and foremost because believing is a normative activity which is shaped by my perception of what is right and reasonable.

This reading of MacKay's argument is then based on the assumption (eminently reasonable) that my beliefs about the causes of my beliefs affect my beliefs. If this is so, then it could never be rational for me to take a deterministic attitude towards my own beliefs. My beliefs are not simply events which are causally determined and which I must try to predict. They are formed by me as the result of rational reflection. When I discover that one of my beliefs is the result of some mechanical process, two possibilities occur. (1) Either I give up the belief as a result of this discovery, or (2) the belief will survive as the outcome of a process of reflection which then becomes part of the cause of my holding the belief. Rational deliberation always presupposes that the outcome of my deliberation is undetermined. Where my actions or beliefs are determined, I may attempt to guess or predict what I will do, but I cannot truly decide.

On this interpretation MacKay's argument does indeed show that action which is rooted in conscious reflection is free, by showing that the process of reflection has a self-reflexive character which makes it impossible for an agent to clearly distinguish cause and effect or regard them as fixed. On this view, it seems to me that there is no reason why an onlooker would not be rationally justified in believing the act was free as well. Such an onlooker can easily understand how this process of reflection makes the agent's choice indeterminate. It would even be of great value to an onlooker to distinguish between cases where (1) the individual's choices are determined and the onlooker can predict the outcome and perhaps intervene or manipulate the individual to attain a different outcome, and (2) those cases where the individual has not made up his mind and may be influenced by rational information and argument. The fact that we often find it "works" to view our fellow human beings as causally determined objects helps to explain both the plausibility of determinism and the value of the behavioral sciences. But the fact that we can and do take such a perspective on our fellows does not mean that it is the only possible one. We often regard our fellow human beings as agents who, like ourselves, have the power of free choice. And we observe their actions and respond accordingly.

Thus it seems to me that MacKay's argument can be taken either as establishing only that persons are free in the sense that the soft determinist says persons are free, or else it can be taken as showing that persons are free in a stronger sense, both from the perspective of the agent and the onlooker. The second reading of the argument is the one that I find most appealing, though I do not think this is what MacKay himself intends. On this interpretation there are still two possible perspectives which we may adopt towards an action. We may regard an act as the determinate product of a necessary law, or we may choose to regard an act as the free outcome of rational deliberation. But these two perspectives can no longer be simply identified with the perspective of the agent and the observer, as observers may at times rationally adopt this latter attitude towards agents, and agents may (at times) rightly regard their own choices as determined.

Whether both these models can be applied to the same act is a crucial question. MacKay seems to want to claim that they can, because the two are complementary. It seems to me that this notion of complementary models of human behavior carries with it both strengths and dangers. The danger is one of instability. This instability is only eliminated when the purposes and scope of the various models are clearly delineated and they are brought into some kind of coherent relationship. I believe that this task requires the Perspectivalist to ask concerning the various models in terms of which man can be viewed, "Which of these accounts is more ultimate?" (MacKay has attempted to do this to some extent.)

The difficult metaphysical question as to whether naturalistic, mechanistic accounts of man are destined to replace personalistic conceptions, both religious and nonreligious, cannot be evaded.

humanizers
of science

The last way of responding to the problem of personhood we shall consider centers its critical fire on the underlying philosophy of science which is seen as generating the difficulty. We have bumped up against this philosophy of science innumerable times in our exploration of the sciences that deal with man. However, since the position of the Humanizer of Science can only be understood as a reaction against this view, it is worth our time to scrutinize it once more.

the hypothetico-deductive method

The philosophy of science in question we summarized in Chapter 7 in two propositions: (2a) there is one method which all genuine science employs, and (2b) this method consists of giving law-like causal explanations which are empirically testable. This view of science, which is capable of many variations our summary glosses over, seems to be widely held, not merely by philosophers of science but by many practitioners of science. In its stress on objective verification of theories, it is strongly empirical. And it is a recognizable descendant of the philosophical movement which Comte called "positivism," whose twentieth-century representatives had a marked influence on the development and success of behaviorism in psychology and in the social sciences.

The philosophy of science we are discussing is not, however, wedded to doctrinaire views associated with positivism, and its adherents are certainly not all positivists. Sophisticated advocates of the "unity of science thesis," for example, have long ago moved away from the naive empiricism that characterized some nineteenth-century positivists. They do not claim that all scientific knowledge is derived by induction, for example. Scientific theories are discovered in all sorts of ways, involving human creativity, imagination and even luck. Scientific theories are not mere inductive generalizations, like "All swans are white." Generalizations of this sort do not generate any new knowledge. Genuine scientific theories have the character of extending our knowledge, in the sense that they have implications which may be unanticipated and which certainly go beyond the original data which may have suggested the theory.

Theories then are to be regarded as hypotheses, not generalizations, and a good hypothesis is one from which we can deduce definite, specifiable consequences. Such hypotheses have the form of a "law-like statement," such as "Whenever A, then B." This hypothesis, when conjoined with the actual knowledge that "A" is the case, enables us to deduce "B" as follows:

Whenever A, then B.	$A > B$
A is the case.	A
Therefore B.	B

This logical deduction can be interpreted as a prediction, a test or an explanation, depending upon our point of view. If we know that "A" is the case and we are interested in knowing what will occur in the future, and if we believe the hypothesis is a good one, then this deduction gives us a prediction. If we actually test to see if "B" does in fact occur, we are engaged in verifying or testing the hypothesis. And if "B" has already occurred and we are interested in giving an explanation of its occurrence, the deduction will serve in this capacity as well. Thus the logical structure of prediction, verification and explanation turn out to be identical. The difference between a prediction and an explanation has to do with our temporal relationship to the event. The theory which generated a prediction will also serve as an explanation.[1]

This view of science, sometimes referred to as the hypothetico-deductive method, makes a sharp distinction between what is called the context of discovery and the context of justification. When its advocates speak of the unity of scientific method, it is the method of justification which is referred to. Scientists may arrive at their discoveries by any method they wish: by dreams, imagination or disciplined experiment. It is, however, necessary to submit all theories to the empirical test of the hypothetico-deductive method. Only when justified in this manner does a theory become a theory of science.

This view of science has been developed and modified in important ways by its advocates. A scientific theory is now generally regarded not as an isolated statement but as a systematically connected set of statements. When viewed in this way it is not necessary to demand that every single statement be verifiable, but only that the set of statements should, as a whole, make contact with experience at certain points.

Karl Popper has gone so far as to suggest that scientific theories are not really verifiable at all. That is, there is no way of conclusively establishing the correctness of a theory. Rather he views the scientific experiment as an attempt to *falsify* a theory. A theory which passes the test has not been conclusively verified, but we are rationally justified in continuing to provisionally accept a theory as long as it continues to "pass."[2]

Even when these modifications are admitted, Humanizers of Science have a bone to pick with this view of science. Like the other two types of views we have considered, however, Humanizers come in two varieties. The first type of Humanizer, the Particularist, does not challenge the appropriateness of the hypothetico-deductive method for the natural sciences. He claims, however, that the particular sciences that deal with man, particularly those which deal with purposive human actions, are unique and should not pattern themselves on the natural sciences.

The Generalist claims that the hypothetico-deductive method, taken alone, does not accurately describe the structure of any of the sciences. According to him, those who say the social sciences should pattern themselves on the natural sciences may be in for some surprises when they take a close look at those sciences.

Although the theoretical difference between the Particularist and the Generalist may seem clear, the two positions do not actually differ much in their practical implications. That is, they largely agree about what the actual character of the social sciences should be. The Particularist will be happy if the Generalist attack on the neo-positivist understanding of the natural sciences is successful. Such a general attack will give him what he wants—the freedom of the social scientist to be his own man and employ his own unique methods of explanation. Thus the success of the Generalist cause would entail the success of the Particularist cause as well. So it is not surprising that the line between these two views is frequently muddy. We shall discuss people under one rubric who are clearly Humanizers of Science but might with equal justice fit into the other category. In fact it would perhaps be proper to regard the Generalist, not as a distinct type at all, but simply as someone who offers an optional set of supportive arguments to the arsenal of the Particularist.

particularists
Historically, the claim that the sciences of man are unique and should not pattern themselves after the natural sciences goes back to the division which German scholars in the nineteenth century drew between the *Geisteswissenschaften* (sciences of the human spirit) and the *Natureswissenschaften* (sciences of nature). This distinction was commonly drawn among philosophers of an idealist persuasion and others influenced by that tradition. The distinction was sometimes pictured as one which divided the cultural from the natural, the sphere of freedom from the sphere of necessity. In dealing with the sciences of the spirit, frequent reference was made to a special method called the method of *Verstehen*, a word perhaps best translated as empathetic understanding. According to thinkers like Wilhelm Dilthey, no genuine science of human actions and cultures is possible without this type of understanding, an understanding which is unique and has no analog in the natural sciences.

Views very similar to Dilthey's have generated a heated controversy in the field of philosophy of history. R. G. Collingwood in *The Idea of History* claims that human actions (which are the true subject matter of history) are not understood or explained merely by subsuming them under general empirical laws.[3] A human action is different from a mere event and must be understood differently. We understand an act when we understand the agent's ideas about his situation, the purposes of the agent, his beliefs about the means available and so forth. All of these have to do with the mind of the agent.

Empirical generalizations have to do with making clear the inevitability or probability of an event. Explanations of the sort Collingwood claims the historian seeks show the point or purpose of an act. Collingwood is in effect claiming that the historian must constantly rely on *Verstehen*. The good historian is one who is able to understand his subject empathetically. He must be able to put himself in the place of the agent and "re-enact his experience." Events in nature have an outside, but history has an inside which we must grasp to understand it rightly.

Neo-positivists have responded to Collingwood's challenge in a number of ways. Generally they charge that Collingwood has confused a method of suggesting hypotheses with the logical structure of an explanation. That historians commonly do employ the technique of *Verstehen* as a way of discovering hypotheses is admitted. But, according to thinkers like Carl Hempel and Richard Rudner, the hypotheses arrived at in this way must still be tested by empirical evidence.[4] Knowing that an agent was "in state of mind C" does not explain why the agent performed act Y unless we know some law of the form "Agents in state of mind C always (or usually) perform act Y." Without such knowledge, it is claimed, we still do not have a complete explanation of why the agent in fact performed Y.

An argument which I believe is at bottom identical to this dispute among philosophers of history is still going on in the philosophy of the social sciences. This argument is related to the quarrel between those sociologists who champion the use of the "participant-observer" method of study and those who argue that the scientist must take a strictly objective point of view. The former type of sociologist may argue that qualitative observations can be of genuine significance, while his more objective counterpart is likely to stress the importance of quantifiable observations and statistical methods. This dispute is also tied to the concept of *Verstehen* and is often developed with reference to the very significant writings of Max Weber, a German sociologist. This difference is perhaps roughly comparable to the difference in anthropology between (1) those traditions which stress understanding an alien culture in that culture's own terms (such as British social anthropology and traditional American cultural anthropology) and (2) contemporary cultural ecology, which stresses understanding a culture as a homeostatic system ideally describable in quantitative terms.

We have quoted already Durkheim's claim that social relationships are things, objective facts, which are discoverable by objective methods:

I consider extremely fruitful this idea that social life should be explained, not by the notions of those who participate in it, but by more profound causes which are unperceived by consciousness, and I think also that these causes are to be sought mainly in the manner according to which the associated individuals are grouped. Only in this way, it seems, can history become a science and sociology itself exist.[5]

This constitutes a rejection by Durkheim of the method of *Verstehen* (at least in this quote). Regardless of whether he himself consistently lived up to this requirement, it has been accepted by many behavioral scientists as an ideal.

Max Weber, on the other hand, finds sociology without *Verstehen* to be a contradiction in terms:

Sociology ... is a science which attempts the interpretive understanding of social action in order thereby to arrive at a causal explanation of its course and effects. In "action" is included all human behavior when and insofar as the acting individual attaches a subjective meaning to it. ... Action is social insofar as, by virtue of the subjective meaning attached to it by the acting individual (or individuals), it takes account of others and is thereby oriented in its course.[6]

The key point to notice in this quote is Weber's assertion that what distinguishes human actions from other types of phenomena is that they possess "subjective meaning."

To illustrate Weber's view, let us imagine that we have observed a man riding a bicycle who swerves to avoid a pedestrian. We might imagine a similar event in which the bicycle rider did not see the pedestrian or therefore did not consciously attempt to avoid him, but nevertheless happened to miss him by a fortuitous "swerve." In both cases the bicycle swerved, but in the first case an action was performed. In the second case the rider did not act. (He may even have temporarily blacked out.) The difference between the two events lies in the conscious intentions of the riders.

On Weber's view the criterion by which we identify an act as identical to or different from another act is the meaning of the act to the agent. It follows that before we can even recognize the act, we must attempt to understand the act from the perspective of the agent. This entails that the investigation of the structure of meanings which make up the "world" of a particular group of people being studied is a primary part of the job of the social scientist. The good social scientist recognizes the necessity to look at the phenomena under study from the viewpoint of the subjects (the agents) being studied.

Weber does distinguish between adequacy on the level of meaning and causal adequacy. To understand the meaning of an act is not necessarily to understand its cause. Objective phenomena like heredity and birthrate obviously may have an impact on human actions. Nevertheless, even causal explanations are rooted in *Verstehen*:

The recognition of the causal significance of such [objective] factors would naturally not in the least alter the specific task of sociological analysis or that of the other sciences of action, which is the interpretation of action in terms of its subjective meaning. The effect would be only to introduce certain non-understandable data ... into the complex of subjectively understandable motivation at certain points.[1]

A view which is similar to Weber's, but perhaps even more extreme, is expressed by Peter Winch in *The Idea of a Social Science.* Winch agrees with Weber that a distinction must be drawn between events which are purely objective and human actions. He compares the natural event of "thunder" to the human act of "obeying a command."[8] Thunder is a natural event which occurred prior

125

to man's existence and before human beings had a concept of thunder. The concept of thunder and the event are in a sense "external" to each other. However, the act of "obeying a command" did not exist prior to the existence of a group of persons who understood the conception of "an order" and "obedience." If an observer chooses to ignore the way in which the agent or agents he is studying understand these concepts, it is highly possible that he will not describe the act (obeying an order) which was really performed. He may be observing a fictitious world of his own making if he follows Durkheim's methodological prescription.

This does not mean that a person who performs an act always consciously thinks about the concepts which give sense to that action. The person who obeys an order does not necessarily consciously say to himself, "That was a command." But it must at least be possible to do this, in the sense that the person must have an understanding of what a command is.

Winch is arguing that it is a mistake to think that human actions are just *seen*—that they are recognizable independently of a conceptual framework. The scientist who thinks that the work of the scientist is just formulating and testing "law-like statements" fails to see that our ability to discern a law-like uniformity is a function of a shared conceptual framework.

A regularity or uniformity is the constant recurrence of the same kind of occasion; hence statements of uniformities presuppose judgments of identity. But . . . criteria of identity are necessarily relative to some rule: with the corollary that two events which count as qualitatively similar from the point of view of one rule would count as different from the point of view of another.[9]

Now the natural scientist is free to formulate his own rules for identifying the phenomena he is studying, since he is studying objective events. He is free to "carve nature up as he wishes," though some ways obviously seem more fruitful than others. If he wishes to be a scientist, he will learn the rules which other scientists follow, and he will learn to make judgments of identity as they do.[10]

But suppose we wish to scientifically study the behavior of scientists. Science as a form of human activity is itself governed by rules, the rules which aspiring scientists must learn. If we wish to study the behavior of scientists, Winch would claim we must make our judgments of identity in accordance with the rules which the scientists we are studying follow. *Their* rules, not ours, define the object of study. If we ignored their rules, we could not claim that we were studying the "making of hypotheses," "designing of experiments" and so forth, because we could not tell whether what we call "making an hypothesis" would be identical with what they would call "making an hypothesis."

And what is true of science is true of all specifically human modes of activity. If we ignore the framework of meaning in terms of which the persons under study understand their behavior we risk studying a fantasy world which does not exist. And Winch would agree with Collingwood and Weber that this framework of meaning is one which makes an act intelligible in terms of its point or purpose rather than in terms of some general law.

Winch would claim that the necessity for taking the subject's point of view does not limit the social scientist to introspective methods. The framework of meaning which he seeks to understand and employ in his observations is by no means subjective in the sense of being private. Two people involved in giving and obeying an order presuppose that each of them understands the other. The conceptual framework in which agents understand their own behavior and the behavior of others is not private, but a publicly shared framework that is learned in a social context.

The practical implications of this are that the genuine social scientist can never abandon or repudiate the perspective of the agent. The social scientist can add new theoretical constructs, but these must be logically tied to the concepts already possessed by those he is studying. On Winch's view the main job of the social scientist is to make behavior intelligible in terms of the values, purposes, intentions, norms and beliefs shared by the group he is studying. The social scientist can make predictions, but his predictions can never be regarded by him as infallible for two reasons. First, human behavior is rule-governed and to understand how to follow a rule is also to know how to disobey it. Second, when someone is following a rule we cannot predict how he will interpret the rule with absolute precision, particularly in new or unusual circumstances. Where a decision is called for, prediction may fail; otherwise it would not be a decision.

With Winch's help we can now formulate a possible reply which Collingwood and Weber might give to their positivist critics. In speaking of *Verstehen* Collingwood was not saying that the historian must be an introspective psychologist. Nor is *Verstehen* merely a heuristic device or source of hypotheses. *Verstehen* is a way of referring to the fact that the social scientist must take a viewpoint close to the acting subject he is studying. Without taking this point of view the scientist will neither be able to observe correctly the actions he is studying nor understand them. The connection between an action and its subjective "meaning" is an essential one. Someone who fails to understand the purpose or point of an act fails to understand the act. And the objection that such "explanations" do not show why the act was inevitable beg the question by assuming that actions *are* inevitable. The advocate of *Verstehen* can argue that when an action "makes sense" to us in the sense that we understand it in terms of the agent's values, purposes and beliefs, no further explanation is needed and perhaps no further explanation is possible.

This movement to humanize the social sciences has its counterpart in psychology as well. The multitude of countermovements to the dominant mechanistic psychologies certainly have to be understood as fitting this category. Although these countertrends differ radically among themselves, they have all been designated by Abraham Maslow as a "third-force" in psychology, meaning that they constitute an alternative to both orthodox Freudian and behavioristic psychologies. This group includes such psychologists as Maslow himself, Carl Rogers, Gordon Allport and Kurt Goldstein. The original defectors from Freud (Adler particularly) and other neo-Freudians, such as Erich Fromm, who have attempted to humanize psychoanalysis, also probably belong in this category. And the distinct though related movements to produce "existential psychology" and "phenomenological psychology" are even more typical. Maslow expresses what is common to all of these diverse groups:

Many sensitive people, especially artists, are afraid that science besmirches and depresses, that it tears things apart rather than integrating them, thereby killing rather than creating. None of this I feel is necessary. All that is needed for science to be a help in positive

*human fulfillment is an enlarging and deepening of the conception
of its nature, its goals and its methods.*[11]

What all of these humanist psychologies have in common is an
emphasis on the person as a unified self or agent, the significance
of choice in human life and the crucial role of values in both science
and life. All have stressed the need in psychology for methods of
research and conceptual frameworks that do not destroy or seriously distort this view of the person.

Some special comment on the idea of existential psychology is
perhaps in order. Many of those termed existentialists, particularly Kierkegaard, the man generally credited with having (uninten-
tionally) originated the movement, would have been uninterested
in the project of the Humanizer of Science. On their view, the
crucial thing is rather to recognize the limits of science and to perceive that self-understanding is not something which can be acquired through a textbook or passed from one person to another as
"objective knowledge." Many of the writings of existential writers,
however, are concerned with the *self* and its central problem: how
to find meaning in a world which sometimes seems to countenance
despair.[12] Hence it is not surprising that these insights have been
appropriated by psychologists imbued with the humanizing ideal.

Existential psychology, as represented by such writers as Rollo
May, is pre-eminently a psychology of the agent. Existentialists
emphasize the pervasiveness and importance of the individual's
free choices. The concept of the individual as a machine which
must be "adapted" to its environment is the concept of an individual who is psychologically sick. The healthy individual possesses
a measure of transcendence and autonomy; he grapples with decisions and does not merely bend to environmental and societal
pressures. The normal anxiety which accompanies such choices is
not a symptom of unconscious sexual problems or anything else;
it is one of the signs of health. The problems an individual has
may actually be due to his bad choices. The existential therapist
regards his patient, not as a case to be diagnosed and prescribed,
but as an agent—another person to be encountered and helped
through mutual dialog.

Some comment on the movement known as "phenomenology" is
also in order, if only because the term is so often misunderstood.

129

Actually, I believe that phenomenology is more accurately discussed under the rubric of the Generalist, since phenomenologists typically claim that phenomenology provides an essential foundation for all the sciences. Nevertheless, since the movement is so often associated with existential psychology, it is appropriate to mention it in this context.

Phenomenology as a philosophical movement originated in the work of Edmund Husserl (1859-1938), a German philosopher. Phenomenology was for Husserl an attempt to return to and describe immediate or "lived-experience." Phenomenology is therefore in a loose sense psychological, because it is concerned with "consciousness." However, it is a great mistake to equate Husserl's views with those of the introspective psychologists who were his contemporaries. These introspective psychologists regarded consciousness as a private, subjective phenomenon—distinct from the objective world. Phenomenologists, however, regard consciousness as the *activity* of apprehending or reaching out to that world, which after all, can be known to me only insofar as I am conscious of it. Whenever I am conscious, I am conscious *of* something. "All consciousness is consciousness of. . . ." The phenomenologist expresses this by claiming that consciousness is *intentional*, meaning that every conscious act has an object which it *means* or intends. Thus for the phenomenologist, consciousness has a double aspect. As an act of consciousness it is subjective, but it also is *about* something which is objective. The phenomenologist tries to focus his attention on these acts of consciousness and thereby describe not only the self but the world as perceived by the self.

What is important to see here is that phenomenology is not, as many psychologists think, simply a revival of introspective methods, such as those rejected by the behaviorists. The cover of a significant book in psychology, *Behaviorism and Phenomenology*, provides an example of this type of misunderstanding, with its assertion that phenomenologists claim that "it is impossible to 'know' the subjective world of another individual."[13] This is precisely what phenomenologists *deny*. If it were impossible to "know" the subjective world of another individual, then the behaviorists would be right and phenomenology would have no value to psychologists.

What the phenomenologist is really suggesting is not so far removed from the perspective of Winch and Weber. It is that the world as experienced by the agent, the "life-world" or world of meanings, is a social, public world which is open to inter-subjective experience. The phenomenologist denies that when I perceive another person's actions I perceive patterns of physical motion. The other person's act is experienced at the outset as meaningful. Alfred Schutz, the phenomenologist who has done the most to make clear the implications of phenomenology for the social sciences, makes this point:

The social world is experienced from the outset as a meaningful one. The Other's body is not experienced as an organism but as a fellow-man, its overt behavior not as an occurrence in the space-time world, but as our fellow-man's action. We normally "know" what the Other does, for what reason he does it, why he does it at this particular time and in these particular circumstances. That means that we experience our fellow-man's action in terms of his motives and goals.[14]

Schutz is claiming that our everyday experience of our fellows is experience of fellow agents and that this experience is no more "private" or "subjective" than other kinds. There is an experiential basis for social sciences which attempt objectively to understand and explain human actions in human terms. In fact, without this everyday awareness of the other as a personal agent, even behaviorist science, which is a communal activity, would be impossible. That is, the behaviorist scientist who writes papers about human beings as stimulus-conditioned organisms writes those papers for scientists whom he assumes are conscious, rational beings, able to perceive and understand the meaning of his words and deeds and respond in rationally appropriate ways.[15]

To summarize, Particularists of all types believe that the central model for the sciences that deal with the person should be the model of the person as conscious agent. They resolve the tension between the image of the personal and science by importing the image of the personal into science. From this perspective, there is no one method which makes a discipline scientific. Rather the rational procedure is to allow the subject matter to determine what methods of explanation are appropriate. In the case of human actions, we are confronted with a subject matter which calls for unique, personal modes of explanation which do not nullify but actually employ the concept of *choice*. Explanations in terms of deterministic causal laws may be appropriate in the natural sciences which deal with mere events, but not in the human sciences that deal with action.

generalists

The Humanizer of Science whom we have termed a Generalist finds little to quarrel with in the conception of the social sciences held by the Particularist. However, he believes that the Particularist makes his case weaker than it really is if he admits the validity of the positivist account of the *natural* sciences. The Generalist believes that a proper understanding of the natural sciences will show that the humanist social scientist is not asking for any "special treatment." All science on his view is a form of "personal knowledge," to use Michael Polanyi's phrase. The notion that science is a value-free, presuppositionless endeavor carried out by detached observers is a myth. The case for the Generalist is one which has been made by the revolution in the philosophy of the natural sciences which has occurred in the last twenty years or so. This revolution, still controversial, has been carried out by such thinkers as Polanyi himself, historians of science such as Thomas S. Kuhn and philosophers such as Stephen Toulmin and Paul Feyerabend.

These thinkers have attacked the positivist view of science right at its heart. Their fire has centered itself around the key concepts of explanation and verification. We shall examine their thinking on each of these two concepts in turn.

The hypothetico-deductive method, outlined at the beginning of this chapter, claims that the logical structure of an explanation is the same as that of a prediction. This equation is very popular among philosophers of science of an empirical bent. It is however questionable to say the least.

The most striking examples of predictive technique ... are the mathematical techniques used to predict the times and heights of tides, the motions of heavenly bodies, and so on. Yet ... some of the most successful techniques for making such predictions have largely lacked the power to explain the events so forecast, having been

*worked out by trial-and-error and without any theoretical basis;
whereas some respectable theories about the very same natural happenings have been predictively almost entirely fruitless.*[16]
Stephen Toulmin also reminds us that the ancient Babylonians
were masters at predicting the times and dates of astronomical
events, but seem to show no ability or even interest in giving what
we should term explanations of these events. The ancient Ionians,
on the other hand, though far inferior as forecasters, are recognizable ancestors of modern science with their speculations and
theories about the heavenly bodies.[17] On Toulmin's view, what is
crucial to scientific explanation is that we possess general notions
and principles which *make sense* of observed regularities in the
sense of introducing coherence where previously there was only
brute fact.

Toulmin believes that the attempt to produce explanations of
this sort is dependent upon the prior possession of what he calls an
"ideal of natural order." The idea here is roughly that certain types
of behavior among natural objects are regarded as "natural," un-
exceptionable, requiring no explanation. The scientist is interested in phenomena which in some way *deviate* from this standard
pattern, an anomaly or irregularity. Such anomalies require an
explanation which will consist of an account of why this particular
deviation (and others) occurred. Without an ideal which makes
some phenomena "irregular" the scientist does not even know
what to look for in the welter of perceptions which confront his
senses.

*The scientist ... begins with the conviction that things are not just
happening ... but rather that some fixed set of laws or patterns or
mechanisms accounts for Nature's following the course it does, and
that his understanding of these should guide his expectations. ...
He does not (and should not) approach Nature devoid of all prejud-
ices and prior beliefs.*[18]

The interesting thing is that these ideals of natural order *change*
in the course of science. Hence what is regarded as an anomaly in
need of an explanation in one era (continuous movement in a
straight line) is regarded in another as precisely the kind of motion
which needs no explanation.

Toulmin's view of science here is close to that popularized by

T. S. Kuhn in *The Structure of Scientific Revolutions*. Kuhn speaks of "paradigms" rather than "ideals of natural order," but the fundamental concepts seem very similar. On Kuhn's view "normal" science requires a shared paradigm. In this phase of science, efforts are directed towards making nature "fit" the paradigm. Fundamental change in science is not the result of gradual accumulation of knowledge but a revolution in which one paradigm displaces another. These paradigms are not simply "observed." In fact, frequently what is observed is very divergent from what is regarded as normal behavior (as in the case of inertia). The paradigm makes meaningful observations possible, by providing form and structure to the perceived world.

We have here moved from the concept of explanation to the second concept which is challenged by the "new" philosophy of science, the concept of verification by observation. This is the key to the neo-positivist case. Kuhn and Toulmin imply that paradigms or "ideals of natural order" are in a sense prior to observation, that they make observations possible. Paradigms are not simply verified or refuted on the basis of observations because scientists who hold two different paradigms may not "see" the world the same way.

Looking at a contour map, the student sees lines on paper, the cartographer a picture of a terrain. Looking at a bubble-chamber photograph, the student sees confused and broken lines, the physicist a record of familiar subnuclear events. Only after a number of such transformations of vision does the student become an inhabitant of the scientist's world, seeing what the scientist sees and responding as the scientist does.[19]

The student who is learning to see the world in this way is being initiated into a paradigm. The point is that observations are contaminated by theory. All seeing is a seeing something as something, to use N. R. Hanson's phrase.[20]

What is the significance of all this for the social sciences? Perhaps this will be made clearer if we examine the sort of criticism which social scientists of a mechanistic bent often make of personalistic explanations of behavior. Suppose it is suggested that a certain person has chosen to join a particular political party. When asked to explain the choice, the person cites certain reasons and beliefs which he holds. A Skinnerian would respond that such an account is not a genuine explanation. Such inner events, he would say, are devoid of predictive power. What is needed is an account of the contingencies which work to reinforce this particular kind of behavior and which presumably were operative in this specific case.

From the perspective of a Kuhn or Toulmin, a new perspective on this claim can be gained. The Skinnerian is operating with an ideal of natural order or paradigm. That is, he has a certain conception of what constitutes an explanation and what constitutes mere data which demands an explanation. On this view to talk of the person's reasons is not to explain the behavior, because a valid explanation will be of the form, "In condition C, Response R will occur."

However, it is perfectly possible for a Humanizer of Science to challenge this paradigm. Suppose our ideal of natural order is "an act done for good reasons." If we ask the person why he joined the party and if his reasons seem good to us, then no further explanation of his behavior is deemed necessary. Indeed, explanations in terms of general laws satisfactory to the Skinnerian will now be regarded as anomalies in need of explanation. If we are told that "response R occurs in condition C," it makes perfectly good sense to ask "*Why* would a person choose to respond in that way on that occasion?"

If all science is rooted in presuppositional paradigms, then the Humanizer of Science need not be apologetic about having one of his own, rooted in the concept of agency, or afraid to point out that mechanistic sciences of man are likewise dependent on such paradigms, which are open to challenge. And the Humanizer will point out that the dispute between his own type of science cannot be settled by any simple appeal to "observation" or "the facts" because the choice of a paradigm largely settles at least the kinds of facts that are perceivable. All scientific observations presuppose a paradigm which is embodied in the practices and beliefs of a community of investigators. What the Humanizer must claim is that the conceptual framework of the agent provides a foundation for genuine scientific work, making possible rigorous intersubjective verification.

difficulties of humanizing science

Like the other two ways of dealing with the problem of "saving the personal," the Humanizer is not without his problems. First and foremost among these is preserving the integrity of science. Does the notion of diverse paradigms so relativize science as to make the ideal of objective truth impossible? It would seem that perception cannot be entirely theory-laden; otherwise paradigms would never "break down" and generate the need for a scientific revolution. It therefore seems that qualifications must be added to keep such a view from degenerating into a relativism. Furthermore, it must be strenuously insisted that the perspective of the agent is not one which is totally culture-bound. Otherwise, Winch's thesis that explanations of behavior must be couched in terms of concepts intelligible to the agent could be taken as implying a complete cultural relativism, so that people from diverse cultures could not even communicate, much less understand and evaluate each other's behavior.

A second area of criticism concerns the relationship of such a humanist science to its mechanistic counterparts. Most observers would claim that these mechanistic sciences have at times succeeded in explaining human behavior. It might be argued for example that Winch's view seems to assume that individuals or cultures always do act for reasons, or at least that the reasons for an act are always the real cause. Is it not palpably clear that sometimes the reasons people give for their actions are rationalizations or ideology? Yet these concepts cannot really be applied if we do not allow for the possibility that a person's behavior is best understood, not in terms of his own framework of reference, but a different one.

The Humanizer does have a response to this charge. He may point out that the fact that our reasons are sometimes rationalizations does not mean they always are. In fact if we could not sometimes distinguish good reasons from mere rationalizations, it is hard to tell how cases of rationalizations could be identified. Second, the Humanizer may admit that the individual's conscious purposes may not be his real ones but claim that those real purposes must at least be assimilable into the agent's framework. That is, those "real" causes must at least be capable of being understood by the agent.[21] For example, someone who wished to convince you that your real reason for joining a church was to gain social prestige presupposes that you are able to understand his account. It is easy for the agent to understand what a "desire for social prestige" is and know how joining a church might lend itself to such a purpose.

The problem of the relationship of the humanist versions of psychology and sociology to their more mechanistic counterparts still remains, though. Some Humanizers seem to take a moderate position in which the legitimacy of diverse types of scientific approaches is maintained. On this view, there is a place for both behaviorism and existential psychology. This sort of moderate position seems to me to lead towards that of a Perspectival/Limiter of Science. For this moderate type of Humanizer will be faced with the two main problems of the Perspectivalist: drawing the limits of the mechanistic sciences and showing how these divergent accounts of the same reality can be unified.

When the question is raised as to how Christians might utilize the Humanizer of Science model some interesting options are presented. If the Generalist view of science as rooted in various presuppositional paradigms is correct, then the Christian will keep a keen eye out for presuppositions which conflict with the fundamentals of his Christian faith.[22] He may also consider the possibility of actually attempting to do sociology, psychology, etc., from a consciously Christian perspective. After all, he believes that this perspective is true and therefore expects that it will prove to be fruitful in helping him to view the world.

For example, in a recent book David Lyon has issued a call for a "Christian sociology."[23] Lyon notes that some secular sociologists have come to the conclusion that sociology should be a self-consciously moral endeavor which aims to change society in accordance with its explicit value-system.[24] Christians who have not swallowed the dogma that sociology is a "neutral" science and that detached objectivity is possible in the social sciences should welcome this as a challenge.

The formation of such organizations as the Christian Association for Psychological Studies and the Toronto-based Institute for Christian Studies are evidence that the concern for Christian thinking and Christian presuppositions is growing among Christian scholars. In fact, one's attitude toward the possibility of a "Christian psychology" or "Christian sociology" provides a good test for distinguishing Humanizers from Limiters of Science. Limiters of Science, largely accepting the "unity of science thesis," are cool to such attempts, even when responsibly formulated by serious scholars rather than for sectarian purposes. Certainly a concern for thinking Christianly should never mask intellectual laziness or a fear of facing genuine evidence which has a bearing on disputed questions. No responsible advocate of a Christian psychology or any other discipline would argue that non-Christians have nothing to contribute to the undertaking. Good science always requires an openness to dialogue and to learning from those with whom one disagrees.

Those who do wish to raise the banner of Christian psychology or Christian sociology will no doubt find the work of the Humanizers very valuable. For example, the existential and "humanist" psychologies are at certain points very congenial to a Christian personalism. However, it is as necessary for Christians to be critical of presuppositions here as it is in the case of behaviorism. Many existential psychologists seem to affirm man's total autonomy—his ability to create his own values and form his personality solely by his own efforts. To Christians this may appear to be a denial of man's creatureliness and an affirmation of pride.

Many "humanist" psychologists are forthright in their naturalistic world views. They affirm that persons, with all their personal qualities, are simply the product of a nonpersonal nature. Christians may question whether such a world view ultimately allows us to make sense of the unique aspects of personhood. We shall say more about this in Chapter 12.

recovering the person: thinking christianly about man

11

Having surveyed the terrain, we should now begin to put down some stakes. Which of the three ways of dealing with the problem of the person seems to offer the greatest possibilities for a creative solution?

Before sketching my own answer to this problem, I want to issue a few disclaimers. I certainly do not claim to be able to offer *the* Christian answer to this problem. On such a problem as this, the notion of *the* Christian answer seems to me to be meaningful only to God. All of the three lines of thought I have sketched out could be developed in a recognizably Christian way; all have strengths and none are without problems. My own convictions on this subject are held, as I think any responsible thinker's should be, with great tentativeness. I consider this essay to be a progress report, subject to change and review in the light of criticism and dialogue, increased scientific knowledge and greater understanding of the biblical revelation.

christianity and culture

In tackling any problem which lies at the interface of science, philosophy and religion, there are some prior questions which must be faced, notably the problems of the relationship of faith to reason and Christianity to culture. Our general perspective on these issues cannot but have an impact on the answer we give to the problem of the personal, because this general perspective will largely determine how we go about resolving the particular issue. For example, if we view Christianity and culture as antithetical (Christ is against culture because culture is inherently sinful), then we will be very suspicious of science.[1] Science is obviously, for better or worse, a part of human culture, and if we view culture as largely opposed to Christian faith, we will not be surprised to find that science seems to oppose Christian belief.

To go to the opposite extreme, there are some thinkers so uncritical of human culture as to practically identify the Christian faith with what is "best and highest" in human achievement. For such a person the idea of a "Christian critique of culture" is virtually impossible, and questioning the results or implications of science from a Christian perspective strikes him as a perverse and obscurantist enterprise. He is likely simply to revise or adapt Christian belief and practice in whatever ways necessary to square with the latest in modern culture.

These two extreme views of Christianity and culture manifest themselves in two extreme views of the relationship of faith to reason. The Christian thinker who says, "I believe because it is absurd" understands the relationship of faith and reason to be largely one of antithesis. On the other end of the spectrum there is the Christian who, trusting in the full reliability of human reason (created by God after all), simply modifies his Christian belief to conform with what seems scientifically or philosophically respectable. Between these two views there obviously lies a spectrum of possibilities.

In dealing with these issues, it is essential to keep three fundamental Christian doctrines in mind and in balance. These are the doctrines of creation, sin and redemption. The Christ-against-culture position, which sees the relationship of faith and reason solely in terms of antithesis, has a strong sense of the pervasiveness of sin but lacks a strong doctrine of creation. In focusing on the sinful aspects of human culture, the idea that God is the Creator of all things is forgotten, and so is the notion that man's rational and creative abilities are God-given gifts. On the other hand, the thinker who identifies Christianity with what is best in human culture clearly has a strong sense of God as Creator but lacks the sensitivity to sin which gives the godly man in both the Old and New Testaments the ability to speak out in prophetic condemnation even of what is "highest" and "respectable" in culture.

The Christian thinker must, therefore, strive to hold these two doctrines in balance—to see the created order, including the order of human culture, as both the good creation of God and as in rebellion against its Creator. When these two doctrines are held together in this tension, the doctrine of redemption takes on its full significance. God in Christ has acted to restore his fallen creation. Those who name Christ as Lord are becoming the advance detachment of this new created order. As new creations themselves, they are to join in the process of redemption, re-creating in Christ the new order of being.

When this redemptive perspective is applied to the problem of faith and reason, it is not enough merely to affirm that faith and reason do not contradict but complement each other. Here faith and reason are still conceived as distinct activities which can be added together. The person who understands faith in terms of the whole person's turning to Christ and sees Christ's work as the redemption of the whole person will see faith and reason as interpenetrating. Faith is, then, trusting commitment to Jesus Christ, a commitment of the whole person which therefore includes the cognitive act of belief. Through this relationship the whole person is forgiven of sin, accounted righteous in the eyes of God and regenerated. That is, he is "born again" and begins the process of becoming what God intends him to be.

One of the crucial areas of his person which participates in this process is his mind. As his mind is informed (in the literal sense) with God's revelation by the work of God's spirit, he begins to think Christianly. This increased rational understanding gives him the ability to understand his own commitment to Christ and his relationship to God in a deeper way. The whole process is dialectical. Faith seeks understanding and leads to it. Understanding generates faith and deepens it.

The thinker who views the relationship of faith to reason this way will apply this dialectical method to problems posed at the interface of science and religion. He will not ignore the data of biblical revelation, nor will he slight the general revelation provided through science and reflection on human experience. Nor will he simply add these two together. He will strive to understand the findings of science within the context of a biblical world view. This may in some cases (but only some) even affect how science itself is "done." In terms of Toulmin or Kuhn, the Christian will probably find some paradigms in the social sciences more plausible and consistent with his world view than others.

But the dialogue goes in the other direction too. Understanding deepens and modifies faith. The redemptive thinker will also strive to interpret the biblical revelation in a way which is consistent with scientific truth. A commitment to the authority of Scripture does not entail a commitment to the infallibility of human exegesis and hermeneutics. Thus even where Scripture explicitly speaks about human nature, it is possible for scientific advances to deepen and modify our understanding of scriptural teachings.

in the image of God

From this perspective, in order to think Christianly about our original question—how to resolve the problem of the person—it is essential to reflect seriously on the biblical data. What is the biblical view of man? (Of course, here and throughout this discussion I mean man as male and female.) It is obvious that no really adequate answer to such a question can be given in a few paragraphs. What I shall attempt is therefore by no means a well-worked-out, comprehensive review of the biblical account. I shall simply try to sketch out what seem to me to be the major features of the biblical picture. If you will, I am attempting to assemble some "reminders" of biblical teachings so fundamental that any account of the person which presumes to be Christian must pay attention to them.

First and foremost, the biblical view of man begins with God. Although our human limitations require us, no doubt legitimately, to conceive of a personal God in terms of our familiar experience of finite persons, there is no doubt that an adequate understanding of man proceeds from an understanding of God, rather than vice versa. The Bible begins with God and his creative activity and ends with the culmination of God's redemptive activity. Everywhere in between, God as providential Creator and Redeemer is constantly in evidence. Hence the first "reminder" which we must emphasize is simply that human beings are a creation of God. Both man's nature and destiny must therefore be understood as rooted in God's creative activity and purposes. This must be understood as implying not simply that God originated human existence (although this is significant) but that the relationship of man to God is one of continual dependence. Apart from God's creative power and activity man is literally nothing.

As a created being, man must be understood as a *creature*. In his creatureliness he is at one with the rest of God's creation. "Then the LORD God formed a man from the dust of the ground" (Gen. 2:7).[2] In Genesis 3:19, the Lord tells Adam that he was taken from the ground: "Dust you are, to dust you shall return." No Christian view of man can afford to ignore the fact that man is solidly part of nature. That man is dust, a bodily creature, makes this especially evident. It is bodily existence which serves as a forceful reminder of man's general creatureliness and the limitations which go with that status.

Man is, however, not merely a creature but a very special type of creature, and it is here that the biblical emphasis falls: "Then God said, 'Let us make man in our image and likeness.' . . . So God created man in his own image . . ." (Gen. 1:26–27). Creatureliness refers to all those ways in which man is essentially different from God. The *imago Dei* refers to those ways in which man nevertheless resembles God. It is these aspects which demarcate man as a personal being, and it is to them we must pay special attention.

The Genesis account does not tell us what the image of God consists of. Much debate has been expended in determining whether the image of God refers to man's rational capacities, or moral capacities, or social capacities and so forth. However, it seems plausible to me that all of these capacities are interrelated in the most complicated way, and that it is therefore a mistake to identify the *imago Dei* with one of them. For example, the ability to love another person certainly presupposes the ability consciously to recognize that person. It seems to me that the image of God consists of that complex unity of activities which are distinctively and uniquely human. These activities must not only be unique to man in the created order; they must also be God-like in the literal sense of resembling those activities through which God has made himself known. Probably no completely adequate account of these special created human capacities can be given. No list will completely escape the charges of failing to be exhaustive and/or being redundant in some respects. The following, however, is my attempt.

Central to the image of God is the concept of action. God is a God who does things, who makes decisions in accordance with his plans and purposes and carries them out. Similarly human beings are first and foremost agents. Their lives do not consist merely of a string of happenings or events, but constitute a series of choices and decisions about what they will do.[3] As agents, humans possess an essential unity. They are not to be conceived as a series of isolated or disconnected events but as self-shaping beings who bear the consequences of previous choices and strive to achieve future ideals. The concept of an agent is not the concept of a part but the concept of the self as a unified whole. This unified wholeness is pre-eminent and takes precedence over whatever account is given of "body, soul and spirit."

To this concept of man as agent a list of very important qualifying adjectives must be added: purposive, valuing, rational, morally responsible, social, passionate, creative and no doubt others. To understand actions one must understand the *purposes* and intentions which these acts express. These purposes are many and various; they certainly include God's command to exercise dominion over the rest of the created order: "Be fruitful and increase, fill the earth and subdue it, rule over the fish in the sea, the birds of heaven, and every living thing that moves upon the earth" (Gen. 1:28). These purposes are rooted in what a person values— what he wants, loves and hopes. A valuing agent is necessarily a *rational* being who has the power both to review and evaluate the worth of alternative courses of action and attempt to calculate the probable outcome of those alternatives by gaining knowledge of the causal mechanisms of nature. Biblical man is not seen as a totally autonomous valuing agent, however, but one called to behave in accordance with God-given values and principles. As such he is *morally responsible*.

Nor is biblical man a self-sufficient, isolated agent. Though he is an individual agent, he is bound up in social relationships in a twofold way. First, he is a creature with social needs, born to live in community: "It is not good for the man to be alone" (Gen. 2:18). Second, his very character and personality are shaped by his social relationships and their character and quality. This is so from the very outset. In the Genesis story, man breaks his relationship to God and his own character is fundamentally altered. As a further consequence Cain destroys his brotherly relationship to Abel and further degrades his character. The Bible is very far from ignoring the pervasive effects of social relationships on the character and being of the individual. Thus the Scriptures have a strong sense of family solidarity, national solidarity, even the solidarity of the human race. Real concrete human beings are involved with other human beings, and it is impossible to give an account of what it is to be human or how a particular human got to be the way he is without holding these involvements in clear view.

Nevertheless, it is all-important how these relationships are viewed. No one chooses to be born to a particular family or economic group or nation. These classifications represent events which "happen to" people. Nevertheless, the Bible never views a person purely as a passive product of these social roles. He is still, in the midst of these roles, a responsible agent. He becomes what he becomes in the context of these social roles which tremendously limit and weight his options as an agent. Nevertheless, as a rational, responsible agent, he is not merely formed by these social relationships; he acts and by acting helps to form these roles in turn. He is not only constituted by these relationships; he himself constitutes them. He plays a role in continuing them, modifying them for better or worse, enhancing or degrading their quality and character.

In all of these contexts human beings are creative. We are not here talking simply of "the arts" as a distinct area of human endeavor, although what is generally referred to as the arts is a striking manifestation of human creativity. We are rather claiming that man has the ability to act creatively and imaginatively in every sphere of human endeavor from science to politics. Creativity and aesthetic sensitivity are not mere additions to humanness; they lie at the very core of the concept. It is no accident that God's fundamental activity is that of creation and that the Greek word for creator (poiētēs) is the root of our English word "poet."

This account of the *imago Dei* is an attempt at representing what is essential to man as a special type of creature. As such it is an "ideal" account. But the biblical record is far from simply an ideal description. It is fundamentally historical. That is, it gives a clear and realistic record of how human beings have actually acted. It does not merely describe man as an agent with the power to choose, but centers on how man has employed that power. Therefore, from a biblical view, although it is important not to view sin as essential to man's being (in that case it becomes a metaphysical necessity, not a moral choice), it is equally important to understand actual concrete man as sinful, in rebellion against God. This sinfulness affects every aspect of the *imago Dei* which we considered.

There is hardly any Christian doctrine more difficult to understand theoretically than the doctrine of "original sin," yet there is hardly any doctrine which seems to have such massive experiential support. The scriptural account of sin is neither mechanistic nor individualistic. It does not regard sin as something which "happens to" a person, nor does it view the individual as a monad who starts with a "fresh slate," uncorrupted by the actions and consequences of actions of his ancestors and the contemporary social environment. Since the Bible has a strong sense of the social unity of man, it is logical that it sees the choices of individuals as having an effect on the larger community. Since the Scripture shows that God has a genuine respect for the integrity of human choice, it is not surprising that the consequences of these choices are allowed full reign, even when those consequences affect others who may be innocent. But sin, like man's social relationships, is never viewed simply as an event which "happens to" people. Human beings are viewed as active and accountable participants in sin. The dialectical view which we saw as characterizing the relationship of the individual to his social environment is present here too. The individual is formed and shaped by sin, which is "original." But he is not a mere product; he is an active, responsible participant in the process.

This account of man as "fallen" provides the context for the decisive redemptive act of God. The biblical picture is that though man is in rebellion against God and does not seek God, God continues lovingly to seek man. The Bible records God's loving attempts to redeem and restore man to his intended place of fellowship with God, climaxed by God's own entry into history. To restore his fallen creatures, God became a human being. He lived and worked among the poor, proclaiming the good news of God's salvation. Dying an innocent death, he rose from the dead to proclaim God's victory over sin and death. Scripture proclaims that through union with Christ, God offers forgiveness and new life to those who repent and affirm Christ as the Lord of their lives.

The new life which a person is promised in Christ is described as "eternal." This concept is not purely quantitative; it does not refer simply to immortality but to a new quality of being that begins here and now. The concept of victory over death is included though. In promising human beings eternal life, God affirms that human beings are intended to have an eternal destiny. The process of creative growth which begins in a man's here-and-now actions does not lead to a dead end.

The Christian concept of "victory over death" is not, of course, equivalent to disembodied existence. The eternal life which is man's intended destiny is a bodily existence. People are made as bodily creatures, and nowhere in Scripture is there any indication that this state is inherently undesirable or is ultimately to be abandoned (although there is much vexation over the problems and limitations connected with our present bodies, marred by the Fall). The resurrection of the body is a pivotal Christian doctrine because it makes clear how intimately unified a person is with his body. That this is so should be neither surprising nor disturbing. After all, God made matter, and he chose to make human beings material creatures. Since human beings are physical creatures, God's salvation would be incomplete were it not for the resurrection of the body.

biblical dualism or biblical monism

This is perhaps an appropriate time to say something of the biblical notions of "soul" and "spirit" and their relationship to the body. Those who have criticized the way dualistic Christians have read into these terms Platonic or Cartesian meanings have a point. The primary biblical emphasis is on the person as a unified agent. In Genesis God does not add a soul to a body to make a person. Rather God breathes on man the physical creature and he (the whole person) "became a living soul" (Gen. 2:7, ASV). *Soul* here refers to a set of capacities—a quality or special mode of existence. The word *spirit* is generally used in a similar way. That is *soul* and *spirit* do not generally refer to "parts" of the person but to the whole person, with special reference to particular capacities which the person possesses.[4] I shall not attempt to say which capacities are "soulish" and which are "spiritual" because I am not sure that the various biblical writers are consistent in their usage. It should be noted that spiritual does *not* denote "nonphysical" as it does in contemporary philosophical parlance. (And of course the biblical concept of "the flesh" which wars against the spirit is not the concept of the body warring against the soul, but the concept of a conflict between two different types of *desires*.)

Having said so much against the dualist reading of Scripture, something must be said against some of the contemporary critics of dualism. The fact that an idea is Greek in origin does not entail its falsity. Those who wish to deny dualism must forthrightly tackle the resulting problems when dealing with life after death and the continued identity of the individual. Actually it seems to me that the Bible neither precludes nor demands dualism. The Bible does not equate the person with the soul or the soul and spirit. The person is the whole man. Neither does the Bible claim that the capacities designated *soul* and *spirit* are completely nonexistent apart from the body. Hence those who regard the idea of a separable soul as a Platonic intrusion upon the Bible cannot claim that Scripture validates their position. The Bible's central thrust is the unity of the whole person as a spiritual bodily creature. (Biblically this does not involve any contradiction.) Hence the emphasis is on the resurrection. But the Bible certainly does not rule out, indeed it seems to teach, some form of continued existence in the period between physical death and the time of the resurrection. It is this continuation of existence after death which the dualist view of the soul as a separable entity is meant to explain. Hence dualism remains an option for the Christian thinker so long as the primary emphasis on the unity of the person is not disturbed.

However, the contemporary Christian thinker is not committed to dualism as his only option, at least not in its traditional forms. It should therefore be no special cause for alarm if future developments in science seem to cut against the dualistic view of the mind as a separate, nonphysical entity. The main strength of the Perspectivalist/Limiter of Science position lies here. This position admits—even stresses—the unity of the person. Thus the fact that a person may be *in some sense* identical with his body is no more cause for alarm than the fact that a poem may be *in some sense* identical with a set of ink marks is alarming to a poet.

of poems and persons
Imagine a poem that has been handwritten with a pen. In a sense the poem is just a set of ink marks. The "ink mark" description of the poem covers all of the poem. There are no parts which do not consist of ink marks. Nevertheless the person who views a poem simply as a set of ink marks is looking at the poem from a definite (and narrow) perspective. Someone else might see a collection of letters of the alphabet; another, an example of poor penmanship; another, a beautiful literary expression of profound emotion.

The key concept here is the concept of identity or sameness. When someone says that the poem is identical with the ink marks, if he means that the two are identical in a strict or absolute sense, his claim is obviously false. Not every property of the ink is also a property of the poem; nor is every property of the poem a property of the ink. Nevertheless, in ordinary life we find it useful to employ looser, weaker senses of identity. That is, we recognize one thing as the same as another if the two have some crucial set of characteristics in common, even if in other ways they differ. For example, a man may be said to be the *same* person he was five years ago, even though he has changed in significant ways and no longer has all the characteristics he possessed five years ago. It is this weaker sense of identity which is being employed when the poem is viewed as identical with the ink marks.[5] The common property which makes the identification plausible is spatio-temporal location. But the poem obviously is more than a set of ink marks; it is a rich, complex unity which can be described from a variety of perspectives.

In a similar way the Perspectivalist wishes to argue that human persons are a complex, rich unity which can be viewed from a variety of perspectives. The fact that a person can be viewed as a body does not entail that a person is only a body. The concept of multiple perspectives on a unitary reality seems to make it possible to save the unity of the person, doing full justice to his bodily character, while avoiding the reductionist denial of personhood. However, when we discusssed Perspectivalism, we noted the problem of relating these pluralistic perspectives to each other. A critic might grant the possibility of plural perspectives and still claim that a reductionist kind of materialism is true because the physical description of the person is the perspective which is more ultimate or foundational. This criticism forces us to ask, "How does one go about determining the ultimacy of a perspective? Which level of description of an object has metaphysical primacy?"

I would offer two criteria to help resolve disputes between rival claimants to metaphysical ultimacy. One is the criterion of comprehensiveness. A perspective which can incorporate other perspectives in the sense that it presupposes those perspectives and then builds upon them seems more adequate than a perspective which cannot illuminate or make sense of any other. The second criterion is the criterion of uniqueness. That perspective seems most adequate which does the most justice to the unique aspects of the entity in question.

When these two criteria are applied to the handwritten poem, the results are interesting. The various levels of description of the poem which are possible seem to form a hierarchy. We noted the possibility of describing the poem in purely physical terms, as a set of ink marks on paper. This description could be made more sophisticated by substituting a chemical analysis of the ink and paper perhaps. Such a description of the poem could be extremely useful in certain circumstances. For example, someone who wished to know whether this poem would be likely to fade and become illegible over a period of time would find this knowledge invaluable. A second level of description would be to view the poem as a collection of letters of the English alphabet; a third would be to view the poem as a collection of English words. Finally someone might describe the poem as a literary creation. Thus we have the following five levels of description:

5 The poem viewed as a literary creation.
4 The poem viewed as words of the English alphabet.
3 The poem viewed as letters of the English alphabet.
2 The poem viewed as ink marks and paper.
1 Chemical description of the ink and paper.

In analyzing these perspectives, the question is not "Which is true?" because they are all possible true descriptions of what might be perceived. The poem *is* a collection of letters, words, ink marks or molecules, depending on the criterion of identity implicit in the particular perspective adopted. The crucial question is which of these levels of description has a better claim if the question of ultimacy is raised.

There is a sense in which the description of level 1 is "basic." This is I think the source of the appeal of reductionist materialism. Each level of description of the poem in a sense presupposes that some description of the poem can be given at level 1. But this by no means entails that the level-1 description is *metaphysically* ultimate. The truth is that, though the poem has a physical embodiment, there is no necessity for the particular embodiment which it happens to have. While certain physical descriptions may be ruled out (one cannot write with water), many others are allowed. The poem could be written with crayon or pencil. The paper could be vellum stationery or a yellow, lined legal pad.

When the two criteria of comprehensiveness and uniqueness are applied, the basis of my stratification of the perspectives becomes clearer. The "alphabet-letter" perspective is more comprehensive than level 2 since it incorporates the "ink-mark" perspective. It is generally known that letters (when written) are composed of a certain material and that ink is suitable for this purpose. Similarly, it is generally known that words are composed of letters and poems of words. In other words that perspective in which the poem is seen as a poem, a literary creation, is most comprehensive. It incorporates all the other perspectives by presupposing them and going beyond them.

The perspective in which the poem is experienced as a poem also scores highest on the uniqueness criterion. There are molecules which do not form ink marks, there are ink marks which do not form letters, there are letters which do not form words, and there are words which do not form poems. Only when a poem is read or heard as a poem does its uniqueness—its character as a *poem*—stand out clearly.

As one might guess, it is my conviction that the case of the poem is closely analogous to the case of the person. Our everyday experience of human beings as persons seems to me to be the perspective which is metaphysically ultimate. In our everyday experience of ourselves and others as conscious agents, we discover what is truly unique about being a human person. This personalistic perspective seems most comprehensive to me as well. That persons should be embodied seems no more surprising than that poems should be embodied.

a model for integration

Therefore, for me the Perspectival/Limiter of Science option offers rich possibilities for integrating contemporary scientific perspectives with the traditional personalistic account. The main problem that may remain is the question a dualist may raise concerning life after death, prior to the resurrection of the body. If the person is in some sense identical with his body, is life after death but prior to the resurrection a real possibility?

To answer this question we must remember that from the Perspectival position, though a person is in some sense identical with his body, he is not merely a body. The person is primarily a conscious agent who performs certain functions. The Perspectivalist holds that this agent happens to be identical at present with a particular body, just as a poem may happen to have a particular embodiment. However it will be recalled that the same poem is capable of embodiment in different forms. Similarly, a human person can undergo bodily changes—plastic surgery, amputation—without ceasing to be the same person. Christians believe that persons whom God resurrects will have radically changed bodies and yet they will continue to be the persons who they are. But is it possible for the person to continue to exist after the death of the old body, prior to the resurrection?

Certainly no philosophical proof can be given that such survival "in-between" is a reality. Having given up traditional dualism, the Perspectivalist cannot put any stock in theories of the immortality of the soul. But it is possible he needs no such theories. After all, the Christian thinker believes that my current existence is due to God's creative activity. I do not exist from moment to moment because I possess a soul but because God wills my continued existence. If God wills my continued existence after my death, could he not maintain it in some form—material or nonmaterial? The question hinges on the conceivability of the thesis, because not even God can perform logical nonsense. (Of course what appears to be logical nonsense to me may not be to God.) So far as I can tell, the idea of survival after death is not logical nonsense. Thinkers of every time and culture have been able to envision the continuation of at least some of their personal functions after death. Does God in fact choose to maintain persons in existence after death? The Bible seems to teach that he does. What form does this existence take? Here the Bible gives no clear teaching. It teaches that at death the believer goes to be with the Lord, but no clear picture of the nature of this existence is given. Speculative answers on this point are possible, but such speculation is probably fruitless except insofar as it serves the purposes of showing the conceivability of survival after death. In any case, such speculation should not detract from the clear scriptural emphasis that the full person is a bodily person and that the destiny of the Christian is the resurrection of the body.

When developed in this way, this view might still be described by some as a form of dualism. For we are asserting that some of the functions and activities of a person could continue after the death of the body. And this is perhaps the major point which dualists wish to insist upon. However, this view differs from at least some traditional versions of dualism. For we are not asserting that these functions and activities are being carried on at present in a non-physical entity called the soul or mind, but rather that some of the functions presently being carried on by the body *could* be carried on independently of the body. In claiming that this is possible, some would argue that we are committed to dualism, because asserting the possible separate existence of the "soulish" functions is equivalent to admitting a distinction between soul and body.

There is support for this claim. Descartes himself at least at one point argues that the soul and body must be distinct because they can be *conceived* as distinct, and whatever can be conceived as distinct *could* exist separately, if God so willed it.[1] That is, he seems to base his claim, not on the fact of the actual separation of soul and body, but on their *possible* separation. If dualism is defined in this way, then my view is indeed dualistic. But this sort of dualism does not seem to threaten the unity of the person. Nor does it seem to be a view which contemporary or future developments in brain physiology could undermine. For even the most hard-nosed reductionist materialists usually only argue that the identity of mind and body is a contingent identity.[7] They admit, even stress, that it is *logically possible* that the mind could be a separate entity and claim only that it is a *present fact* that mind and brain are identical. Even in the face of this hard-nosed position, the Christian's position seems secure. The Christian could here simply assert that after death this logical possibility becomes a reality, without, of course, agreeing with the reductionist claim that consciousness is *only* a set of physical events. For whatever is logically possible is actually possible for God.

It seems to me therefore that the Perspectival/Limiter of Science position offers great promise as a working model for reconciling the contemporary sciences of man with biblical personalism. Such a view allows for a unified view of the person which is congenial to the Bible's emphasis on the unity of the person and the resurrection of the body. This does not mean, however, that I think the other models for integration have nothing to offer. In fact, I think the Humanizer of Science position is particularly helpful. Indeed I am convinced that the differences between the Humanizer and the Perspectivalist are not so great as they might appear and that there is hope that the two views might be synthesized, so long as both sides state their views moderately.

The main difference between them may in the last analysis be essentially semantic. It concerns the question, "What sort of intellectual enterprise deserves the essentially honorific title of 'science'?" No one familiar with the power of words and the prestige of science would want to call such a dispute "merely" one of semantics. But the following points should be noted. First, Humanizers, at least of a moderate variety, do not necessarily deny that there are more restricted methods of investigation which can legitimately and usefully tell us things about man. They merely wish to urge that the scientific picture produced by these methods is fragmented and incomplete and must be supplemented by richer and looser procedures to get a full picture of man. Of course they feel that these methods are equally deserving of the name "science."

Second, Perspectivalists do not necessarily have to deny that the dimensions or aspects of human reality which science, because of its limited perspective, fails to see can be cognitively investigated or reflected upon in some way. Once the bugaboo of scientism is dismissed, we do not have to be afraid to admit that there may be genuine knowledge which is not "scientific" (which does *not* mean unscientific). Perspectivalists are inclined to say that man can be reflected upon as a moral, religious and creative being. Concepts can be explored and beliefs formed in the arenas of theology, philosophy, literature and everyday life. While these arenas may not be judged sciences, they can nonetheless be penetrated by thought. We can in these matters be learned or ignorant, wise or foolish. We can form our opinions for good and bad reasons, and these can be discussed and examined in the critical marketplace of ideas.

The moderate Humanizer and the Perspectivalist, once they realize that their disagreement over the use of the term "science" is not substantive but merely reflects a sensitivity to different (but equally important) emphases, have much to say to each other. The Perspectival/Limiter of Science, with his concern for the integrity of science, can help the Humanizer see the value of rigorous, objective inquiry. The Perspectivalist who appreciates the contribution of the sciences which take an essentially mechanistic view of man helps us to see man's "creatureliness" more clearly. The Humanizer, on the other hand, with his sensitivity for the role which subjectivity and presuppositions play in science, can help the Perspectivalist gain a clearer understanding of his own subjective commitments, and a greater sensitivity to the way presuppositions may shape a particular scientific methodology. It is commonplace among thinkers of a Perspectival bent to say that B. F. Skinner's scientific work is excellent but that in Skinner's popular writings unwarranted extrapolations are made.[8] Without in any way attempting to judge the merit of Skinner's scientific work, I should like to say that this distinction is not easy to draw because the line between Skinner's scientific work and his philosophy of man is more intimate than this comment would allow. The Humanizer of Science helps us to see the importance of underlying presuppositions.

The Christian thinker who is working from a synthesis of the Perspectival and Humanizer positions seems to be in a position to offer a view of the person which does the most justice to the following concepts: (1) the creatureliness of the person, (2) the transcendence of the person, (3) the unity of the person, and (4) the integrity of science.

First, as man is part of the created order, it is not surprising that methods of investigation which have proved fruitful in dealing with nonhuman animals or even nonliving entities such as computers should be fruitful in studying human beings as well. It is my earnest hope that no one has read this essay as an attack on behaviorism or any other scientific approach to human behavior, no matter how mechanistic. I am completely convinced that such scientific approaches offer great promise in dealing with many significant human problems. The more we understand the nonrational mechanisms which govern our own behavior, the more ability we gain to intervene rationally and gain more control (and freedom) over our own behavior. The person who is moody and depressed because of an inadequate diet is a slave to his emotions so long as he is ignorant of their true cause. With knowledge of the mechanisms involved, he gains some ability to control his emotions by changing his diet. Similar points could be made about the person with subconscious hang-ups, the person who is a rigid product of his socio-economic circumstances or the person who is manipulated by clever use of reinforcements. Only knowledge of these causal mechanisms offers promise of greater freedom. The creatureliness of man means that human freedom is sharply limited. Indeed, rather than speaking of "freedom" per se, in most cases it makes more sense for us to speak of the degree of freedom which an act reflects.

Second, the Christian thinker must remember that human beings are not only creatures but creatures made in the image of God. Hence man's transcendence of the mechanical order of nature, though incomplete, must not be lost sight of. Human beings are, like God, conscious agents who make free choices. They are *persons* with all that this word implies, and all forms of reductionism must be eschewed.

Third, these creaturely persons are nevertheless unified. They are not simply a body plus a soul, where soul is taken to be an actual separate entity. As bodily creatures they are persons who bear the image of God. This unity seems best preserved by the sort of model we have sketched out.

Finally, this Perspectival view which has been reconciled to the Humanizer of Science view seems to do the best job of preserving the integrity of science. This model for integration not only respects the rigorous methods of the hard-nosed sciences; it also helps those sciences acquire a perspective on their own presuppositions and values.

Is such a model for integration a viable possibility? It seems to me to be not merely a possibility but a reality. That is, it seems implicit in a great deal of the recent work done by practicing Christian scholars in their respective scientific disciplines. What I have hoped to do in this essay is not to propose a new way of integrating Christian personalism with the human sciences but to help those engaged in carrying out this integration gain a greater self-consciousness about their approach, a greater understanding of the issues and their significance, and a clearer perception of what alternatives there may be. To accomplish these goals even in slight measure would be no mean feat.

12 man in a personal universe

This book has been written from a humanist perspective. The word *humanist* has varied meanings today. I have used it predominantly as a way of referring to myself as a scholar trained in one of the disciplines currently regarded as one of the "humanities." The word carries with it a secondary sense which I have tried to be faithful to as well: someone who cares about human beings and what it means to exist humanly.

The word *humanist*, however, also carries a rather different sense—that of a person whose moral concerns are explicitly non-religious in any traditional sense. Thus in many countries there are active "humanist associations," with various concerns, one of which is usually opposing traditional religion. As a confessing Christian I obviously do not consider myself a humanist in this sense. Nevertheless, it is my sincere conviction that a great deal of what I have written in this essay could be—and should be—accepted by a genuine humanist in this nonreligious sense. Although parts of this book, particularly those concerned with theology or the possibility of life after death, will no doubt seem irrelevant to such a secular humanist, many other parts, including the review of the threat of mechanism (Chapters 1-5), the argument that mechanism cannot be the whole story (Chapter 6) and the review of various strategies for reconciling the human sciences with personalism (Chapters 7-10), may be of great interest to anyone concerned over the status of the person in today's world. Up to this point, this book could be rewritten, either by myself or someone else, from a purely secular point of view, and yet most of the substantive points would remain. It seems to me that on the issue of personalism, secular and religious humanists can walk a long way together and fight many common foes. A theistic and naturalistic humanist may both agree that the value and dignity of the individual requires us to preserve the concept of man as a personal agent.

Nevertheless, it is also my conviction that the question of God is quite relevant to the question of man. That is, I believe that questions about the ultimate nature of man are closely linked to questions about the ultimate nature of the cosmos of which human beings are so obviously a part. There are certain difficulties for a nontheist who wishes to believe that human beings are genuine persons. These difficulties represent temptations for the secular humanist to abandon his faith in the personhood of persons. I believe that it is partly for this reason that many sincere, ethically motivated people (like B. F. Skinner) are driven to abandoning the traditional concept of the person. It is of course possible that these temptations may be withstood, but I believe it is noteworthy that a religious world view gives protection against these traps. This is what I shall attempt to make clear in this chapter.

the tenacity of reductionism
In the last few years a massive philosophical attack on reductionist views of man has developed. It is noteworthy that very little of this literature has an explicitly religious foundation. Stuart Hampshire's *The Freedom of the Individual* and Lewis White Beck's *The Actor and the Spectator* are excellent examples of this type of attack on mechanistic views of the person. What I find particularly striking about this literature is how little impact it has had on the contemporary mechanistic mind. I am not here commenting on the particular criticisms mechanists have addressed against these arguments, but the almost serene conviction on the part of the mechanist that there *must be* some answer to the hu

manist case. Frequently, hard-nosed scientific materialists regard the new personalists as obscurantists holding back scientific progress, resisting the completion of the triumphant naturalist world view. Even those who would like to accept the conclusion of writers like Hampshire and Beck find it difficult to do so.

Why is this so? Why is it so difficult to believe in the personhood of the person? It seems to me that many of these contemporary defenders of personalism are still making the mistake of Descartes. By this, I do not mean to imply that they are dualists, or that they share Descartes' view of the person. What then do I mean?

On Descartes' view, which we discussed in Chapter 2, man is seen as "the great exception" to an otherwise mechanistic universe. Although Descartes was a theist, his God does not seem to play any vital role in creation. (Descartes does, however, rely on God's goodness as Creator to certify the reliability of human reason and sense perception.) God is curiously "external" to his creation in Descartes' universe. The mechanistic explanation of nature seems to be vital; God seems an external appendage. It does not seem a great step from Descartes' universe to deism and finally to a mechanistic view such as La Mettrie's which sees no need of the God-hypothesis at all.

In such a mechanistic universe the status of man as "the great exception" seems inherently unstable. There is an irresistible temptation to complete the mechanistic explanation of reality by "reducing" human beings to the level of the rest of the natural order. It is for this reason that so many contemporary defenses of personalism are unconvincing. Good arguments are assembled to show that persons are not best understood as machines. However the arguments are unconvincing to the convinced naturalist. He cannot make sense of the idea that human beings are an anomaly to an otherwise mechanistic order. How could such a break occur in the evolutionary ladder? How could freedom, choice and consciousness suddenly enter a material, determined world? Thus, J. J. C. Smart, in defending a contemporary version of a materialist view of the mind, simply finds it incredible that

sensations, states of consciousness . . . seem to be the one sort of thing left outside the physicalist picture. . . . That everything should be explicable in terms of physics . . . except the occurrence of sensa-

tions seems to me to be frankly unbelievable.... I cannot believe that ultimate laws of nature could relate simple constituents (mental happenings) to configurations consisting of perhaps billions of neurons.... Such ultimate laws would be like nothing so far known in science.... If any philosophical arguments seemed to compel us to believe in such things, I would suspect a catch in the argument.[1]

As a convinced naturalist who believes that "everything is explicable in terms of physics," Smart finds any account of mental phenomena other than a physical one unbelievable. Perhaps his mistake lies in his assumption that the physicist's account of "everything else" is ultimate. I am not prejudging Smart's claim that the scientific laws discovered by brain physiologists will be of one type rather than another. I am simply pointing out that unless one resists Smart's claim that "everything else" has already been given an "ultimate" explanation, one will likely be forced to agree with his contention that if the physiologist does get around to giving us a complete account of brain functions in terms of the interaction of elementary particles, then that account will also be adjudged "ultimate."

the contribution of christian theism

In the last chapter we sketched a view of the person which we called "perspectival." From this viewpoint, although it is true to say that a person is his body, it is false to say that a person is *only* his body. How is it possible to accept some sort of identity (at least in this life) between a person and his body while denying reductionism? To me it is quite possible because I do not accept the mechanistic description of my *body* as metaphysically ultimate. My body is the form of my being, the incarnation of my conscious intentions. Ultimately it is part of God's creation. Without denying the possibility of a mechanical description of my body, I can deny that such a description is ultimately true in the sense that it supplants or replaces these other descriptions. From a Christian perspective, although human beings are "dust," they are also "living souls," made in the image of God. These two descriptions are by no means contradictory.

Man is manifestly a part of the natural, material order. From a

Christian perspective, that natural material order is *not* best
understood in purely mechanical terms however, although such an
understanding is perfectly legitimate and extremely valuable.
(It is here that the view of science of the Humanizer is so important.) The material universe is the result of God's creative activity,
and it must be understood in the light of God's creative purposes.
For the Christian, nature is the arena for moral endeavor—a
sphere for artistic creativity—as well as the basis for material
existence.

If we understand nature in these terms, then we can admit to the
physicality of human persons without fear of compromising their
personhood. The Christian does not explain personal activity in
terms of physical being. He understands physical being in terms of
personal activity—the activity of God whose being is indistinguishable from his actions. That God chooses to make persons
from matter is neither surprising nor threatening, for matter is an
expression of God's creative activity.

In a theistic universe, personal categories are not mere "surface
phenomena." Persons are not mere anomalies, late fortuitous
arrivals on the evolutionary scene. If God exists, the universe itself is personal to its very core. In such a universe, belief in the
personhood of human beings makes eminent sense. It would seem
then that when one tries to work out a view of man which does
justice to the unity of the person with the body, it makes all the
difference how one views the body. Is the human body merely a
product of time, chance and whatever brute reality must be
accepted as a given? Or is the human body the culmination of God's
creative activity, the means by which God realized his purpose of
making beings who would be enough like him to commune and
fellowship with himself?

The significance of the belief that the universe is personal can
best be seen if we contrast this belief with another. The contemporary French thinker Jean Paul Sartre is perhaps a paradigm
of a thinker who rejects religious faith in favor of atheism, while at
the same time attempting to view human persons as free beings
who are not mere products of their environment. Sartre's philosophy is a protest against every attempt to degrade man and see
him as a "thing" or set of functions.

According to Sartre, atheistic existentialism implies that man's existence precedes his essence. "There is no human nature, since there is no God to conceive it."[2] God's nonexistence implies that man is free, autonomous. The individual can choose to be whatever he makes of himself through his free choices.

But does Sartre's atheism logically lead to his belief in human freedom? Simply because man is not a product of God, does it follow that man is not a product of anything? Is it not more logical to conclude that, if there is no God, man is the product (ultimately) of matter, time and chance? In such a universe man appears as a mysterious "upsurge of freedom," to use Sartre's own words. While such an "emergence" may be conceivable, such a break in the evolutionary chain hardly seems reasonable. I suspect this is why most naturalistic thinkers do not follow Sartre in his defense of freedom. By contrast, in the context of a personal universe man's appearance, whether sudden or gradual, is no anomaly. Man can be understood as the apex of the created order. The believer feels at home in the universe because he sees it as "my Father's world."

No final proof can be offered that human beings are genuine persons. The fact that human beings are "dust" means that it is possible to regard them as mere objects in the natural order. And as we noted in the previous chapter, for many purposes it is both legitimate and valuable to do so. Even Martin Buber, in the course of developing his famous distinction between "I-thou" and "I-it" relationships notes the necessity for relating to others at times as "its" or objects. "And in all the seriousness of truth, listen: without It a human being cannot live." But Buber is quick to add, "But whoever lives only with that is not human."[3]

But *are* human beings persons who can rightly be related to as "thou's"? Is not the question of man's status in the final analysis a scientific question, to be settled by an appeal to facts? Regardless of how much we wish to regard ourselves as personal agents, are we perhaps engaging in a form of self-deception founded in wish-fulfillment if we do?

The answers I have to give to these questions are largely outlined in Chapter 6, and the reader who finds the above questions troubling is urged to reread that chapter. But a little more remains to be said.

agents and observers

Let us consider once again the distinction between two attitudes which we adopt in our daily existence, the attitude of the scientific observer and the attitude of the agent. To illustrate this distinction imagine yourself as a worker in a scientific laboratory. You notice that one of your fellow workers is pilfering supplies. The first question you might ask is "Why has he done this?" To gain an answer you might find it helpful to adopt the attitude of a detached observer. To this end you might investigate the person's socio-economic status, family history, psychological peculiarities. In some cases, you might find it helpful to assume that the person in question does not himself understand his behavior or its true causes. (This is not the *only* way of observing him, of course.)

However, "Why did he do it?" is not the only question which faces you in this situation. There is also the question, "What should *I* do about it?" Shall I confront the person? Shall I report his behavior to our superior? Shall I call the police? Shall I ask for a share of the take? Shall I do nothing? In raising these questions I am assuming the standpoint, not of a detached observer, but of an agent.

All human beings (including scientists) are both observers and agents. They could never be observers if they were not sometimes agents, and they could never be agents if they were not sometimes observers. If we were not able to observe the world, we would hardly be able to act meaningfully in it. But it is noteworthy that scientific observations are made possible by doing something—by operating on the world. Even simple observations often are the result of the activity of looking for or at something. As observers we sometimes observe our fellow observers and agents. We observe them in a variety of ways, sometimes (but not always) very much in the same way that we observe trees and stones and molecules.

There is nothing illegitimate about this. It is simply true that sometimes the conscious purposes and beliefs of the observer-agent we are observing are not genuinely causally effective. Sometimes persons act in ways which can be predicted if the observer knows something about the brain physiology or class structure or early childhood of the person being observed, even if the person himself is unaware of the importance of these factors. So we ignore the personal character of the person being observed. (Let me

165

hasten to repeat that not all observation is of this sort.) We try to understand his behavior as we would any other object in the natural order, and our efforts may succeed. We may even help the person under study gain a new self-awareness, to help him become more personally responsible for his acts.

This type of observing of the other, whose roots are found in our ordinary dealings with one another (He doesn't really know why he does that, but an objective observer can see . . .), represents in embryo form the human sciences. Developed, magnified, governed by rigorous norms and methods, we discover more and more about man as object. The critical question then is, "Can a conception of man which sees him as an object in the natural order, part of a causal mechanism, be the *whole* truth?"

If we radically change our perspective and reflect on what it is to be a person acting, a very different picture emerges. What is crucial is that we do not merely *observe* man acting but consider what it is to be a person from the viewpoint of the *agent himself*. The person faced with a choice or decision cannot simply step back and *observe* himself making the decision. He cannot simply reflect on his past or his genes or his social relationships with a view toward *predicting* his decision. He must *make* the decision. As he deliberates, he must presuppose that he has a choice which he can make well or poorly. That he is free, that some decisions are better (more valuable) than others, are the necessary presuppositions of meaningful choice. The personalistic conception of man may not emerge as the outcome of an empirical investigation of human actions toward which we take an essentially objective stance; this is why it is naive to regard the question of man's ultimate nature as a mere scientific question of "fact." But that personalistic conception is the everpresent background which we constantly presuppose when we ourselves act.

So which conception of man must we opt for? Shall we view ourselves purely as objects, or shall we affirm the conception of man which we presuppose in the act of choosing? The answer to this question is implicit in our initial remarks on man as observer-agent. Observing is itself an activity, and it is an activity which can only take place if man engages in other activities as well. Science itself is a human activity which presupposes that the one pursuing the activity is a valuing, and to some extent rational, agent. No true account of man could be derived from science which makes the existence of science itself as a form of human activity unintelligible.

This insight is hardly novel; it has long been recognized by philosophers. What we are affirming is what Kant termed the "primacy of the practical," and what Kierkegaard would have termed the primacy of existing over knowing. To affirm the primacy of living and doing over objective thinking and knowing is by no means to reject or minimize the importance of objective thinking and knowing. It is simply to note that thinking and knowing are personal activities, and to set them within their proper context, the context of agency. Scientists do not simply happen to be persons in addition to being scientists. Being a scientist is itself a form of the personal, a way of being-in-the-world. The scientist who repudiates the reality of the personal on the basis of his scientific work is involved in what I should call a practical self-contradiction. He interprets his findings in such a way that they contradict the beliefs that his actions as a scientist necessarily commit him to. Even the person who denies the significance of the personal affirms it to the extent that his denial is a significant act.

The person who demands that we abstain from believing that we are persons because such a belief is seen by him as self-deception is still *acting* as if he were a personal agent. As a responsible person he is choosing to affirm a value—the value of truth—and telling us that we *ought* to affirm that value as well. Such a stand and such a request make no sense if human beings are not persons—responsible agents who can recognize the value of a course of action and choose to respond appropriately.

To live is to choose. To cease to choose is to cease to live. No conception of man which does not make sense of choosing as seen by the chooser can be finally adequate. Mechanistic science can certainly explain "choices" after a fashion, but these explanations do not make sense of choices from the perspective of the agent. And that perspective cannot be rationally repudiated so long as one continues to *be* an agent.

Someone has said that war is too important to be left to generals. So here we might say that the essential truth about personhood is too important to be left to the sciences. Though scientific knowledge may be tremendously important, one does not need to go to psychology textbooks to realize that one is a person and that to be a person is to be faced with decisions for which one is responsible. Anyone who honestly asks, "What shall I do with my life?" possesses the resources to understand what it is to be a person. And a person who possesses this understanding is at least intellectually ready for a confrontation with the Christian revelation in which the True Person makes himself known. For the biblical account of man's nature, origin, present status and future potential through God's redemptive activity is throughout an account of persons acting responsibly or irresponsibly in relationship to God and their fellow persons.

the reality of the personal

I conclude that it is reasonable to believe in the reality of the personal. I argued earlier that such a belief makes most sense if the universe is itself viewed as personal—the sort of reality envisioned by Christian theology. Of course there are other religions which see the universe as personal as well. But if personalism were not plausible, if persons were only a by-product of impersonal causes, Christianity would be most implausible. Hence the plausibility of personalism renders Christianity more plausible. And if I am correct in arguing that it is difficult to separate the question of man and the question of the cosmos, then if Christian theism is plausible as a world view this renders belief in personalism more credible. Christianity makes personalism plausible and is in turn rendered more plausible by personalism.

From the perspective of Christianity the connection between personhood and faith is still more intimate. For "person" is not simply a title which automatically is earned by a human being upon being born. To be a person is to be an agent, and to be an agent is to be engaged in a quest. Christianity affirms that human beings as responsible agents have the power to choose. The consequences of misusing this power are tragic. The person who misuses his power to make choices may even lose his power to make responsible choices.

Christianity is not simply a world view which makes a particular view of man more plausible. It presents itself to human beings as a way of life which represents the fulfillment of that quest which constitutes personhood. The implications of this are enormous. For we have seen that one does not learn what it means to be a person simply by reading books or acquiring facts but by being a person. Thus the question "Who is Jesus Christ?" can no more be treated as purely theoretical than the question "Who am I?" If the former question is to have any relevance to the latter, it must be asked by the whole person. In a quest for self-knowledge, the quality of striving which characterizes the quest affects not only the possibility of gaining an answer but the content of that answer.

notes

Chapter 1: The Problem: The Attack on the Person

[1] C. S. Lewis, "The Humanitarian Theory of Punishment," *20th Century: An Australasian Quarterly Review*, 3 (1949), 5-12; reprinted in C. S. Lewis, *God in the Dock*, ed. Walter Hooper (Grand Rapids: Eerdmans, 1970), pp. 287-94.

[2] I am *not* saying that no moral questions arise about methods of treatment.

[3] See Thomas Szasz, *Law, Liberty and Psychiatry* (New York: Macmillan, 1963).

[4] C. P. Snow, *The Two Cultures and the Scientific Revolution* (Cambridge: Cambridge University Press, 1959).

[5] B. F. Skinner, *Beyond Freedom and Dignity* (New York: Vintage/Bantam, 1972).

[6] D. M. Armstrong, "The Nature of Mind" in *The Mind-Brain Identity Theory*, ed. C. V. Borst (London: MacMillan, 1970), pp. 68-69.

Chapter 2: Minds and Brains: The Person as Machine

[1] René Descartes, *Meditations* in *Discourse on Method and Other Writings* (Harmondsworth: Penguin, 1968), p. 159.

[2] See, for example, Dean E. Woolridge, *The Machinery of the Brain* (New York: McGraw-Hill, 1963). Keith Campbell, a contemporary philosopher, defends an epiphenomenalist position in *Body and Mind* (Garden City: Anchor, 1970).

[3] See the discussion of Skinner in chapter 4.

[4] See A. H. Turing, "Computing Machinery and Intelligence," in *Minds and Machines*, ed. Alan Ross Anderson (Englewood Cliffs: Prentice-Hall, 1964), pp. 4-30.

[5] Hubert Dreyfuss, "A Critique of Artificial Reason" in *Human and Artificial Intelligence*, ed. Frederick J. Crosson (New York: Appleton-Century-Crofts, 1970), p. 162.

[6] C. U. M. Smith, *The Brain* (New York: Capricorn Books, 1972), p. 35.

[7] See particularly Michael Scriven, "The Compleat Robot: A Prolegomena to

Androidology" in *Dimensions of Mind*, ed. Sidney Hook (New York: Collier/ MacMillan.)

[8]Hillary Putnam, "Robots: Machines or Artificially Created Life?" in *Human and Artificial Intelligence*, pp. 178-202.

[9]See D. M. MacKay, "The Use of Behavioral Language to Refer to Mechanical Processes," in ibid., p. 143. Turing also makes such a claim.

[10]See Michael Polanyi, *The Tacit Dimension* (Garden City: Doubleday, 1966).

[11]See Dreyfuss, "A Critique of Artificial Reason." Dreyfuss' book *What Computers Can't Do* (New York: Harper and Row, 1972) is an excellent general critique of the claims made by workers in the field of artificial intelligence, not only in translation but in pattern recognition and game playing.

Chapter 3: The Loss of the Person in Psychology: Freud

[1]*The Origins of Psychoanalysis: Sigmund Freud's Letters to Wilhelm Fliess, Drafts and Notes*, 1887-1902 (New York: Basic Books, 1954), p. 355.

[2]Sigmund Freud, *An Outline of Psychoanalysis*, 1st ed. (New York: W. W. Norton, 1949), p. 14.

[3]Ibid., p. 15.

[4]Ibid., p. 16.

[5]The business is normally more complicated than this, but the complications do not affect the point I want to make.

[6]Sigmund Freud, *The Ego and the Id* (London: Woolf, 1935), p. 47.

[7]Binswanger's assessment is found in "Freud's Conception of Man in the Light of Anthropology" in *Being in the World*, trans. Jacob Needleman (New York: Basic Books, 1963), pp. 147-81.

[8]Ludwig Binswanger, *Sigmund Freud: Reminiscences of a Friendship*, p. 99, quoted in Rollo May, *Psychology and the Human Dilemma* (Princeton: D. Van Nostrand, 1967), pp. 89-90.

Chapter 4: The Loss of the Person in Psychology: Behaviorism

[1]J. B. Watson, "Introduction" to *Behaviorism*, 3rd ed. (Chicago: University of Chicago Press, 1930), p. v.

[2]Ibid.

[3]Ibid., p. 6.

[4]B. F. Skinner, *About Behaviorism* (New York: Alfred A. Knopf, 1974), p. 3.

[5]Watson, pp. 238-39.

[6]Skinner, p. 16.

[7]Ibid., p. 17.

[8]Ibid., p. 21.

[9]Ibid.

[10]Ibid., p. 17.

[11]B. F. Skinner, *Science and Human Behavior* (New York: MacMillan, 1953), pp. 32-35.

[12]This seems to conflict with his earlier admission of the possibility of introspection.

[13]Skinner, *Science and Human Behavior*, p. 34.

[14]Ibid., p. 35.

[15]Skinner, *About Behaviorism*, p. 21.

[16]B. F. Skinner, "Behaviorism at Fifty" in *Behaviorism and Phenomenology*, ed. T. W. Wann (Chicago: University of Chicago Press, 1974), p. 91.

[17]Skinner, *About Behaviorism*, p. 19.

[18]Skinner, *Beyond Freedom and Dignity*, p. 23.

[19]Ibid., p. 193.

[20]Ibid., p. 39.

[21]Ibid., p. 38.

[22]C. S. Lewis, *The Abolition of Man* (New York: MacMillan, 1965), p. 72.

[23]Skinner, *Beyond Freedom and Dignity*, p. 197.

[24]Ibid., p. 99.

[25]Ibid., p. 130.

[26]Ibid., p. 131.

Chapter 5: The Loss of the Person in Sociology

[1]Émile Durkheim, *The Rules of Sociological Method* (Glencoe, Ill.: Free Press, 1938), p. 14.

[2]Ibid., p. 28.

[3]Ibid., p. 29.

[4]Émile Durkheim, *Suicide* (Glencoe, Ill.: Free Press, 1951), p. 44.

[5]Émile Durkheim, rev. of "Essais sur la conception materialiste de l'histoire" by A. Labriola, *Revue Philosophique* (December 1897), quoted in Peter Winch, *The Idea of a Social Science* (London: Routledge and Kegan Paul, 1958), pp. 23-24.

[6]Peter Berger, *Invitation to Sociology: A Humanistic Perspective* (Garden City: Anchor/Doubleday, 1963), p. 87.

[7]Actually *functionalism* is a term used in a variety of ways by social scientists.

[8]See Berger, p. 41.

Chapter 6: Feeling the Loss: Why Care?

[1]I will discuss in chapter 12 whether the nonreligious thinker has an adequate basis for his belief in the uniqueness of personal being.

[2]I do not wish to claim here that a causal relation is only a regular sequence.

[3]In ordinary language the terms *reason* and *cause* are not always clearly distinguished in this way. In the following account I mean by *cause* an account of an event which can be stated in terms of a law or a law-like statement. By *reason* I mean an account of an event which appeals to the purposes or intentions of an agent.

[4]See especially Chapter 1, "Can a Human Machine Think?" in Lewis White Beck, *The Actor and the Spectator* (New Haven: Yale University Press, 1975); I do not claim he would agree with my formulation of this argument.

[5]B. F. Skinner, *Verbal Behavior* (New York: Appleton-Century-Crofts, 1957), pp. 418-31.

[6]Skinner, *Beyond Freedom and Dignity*, p. 99.

[7]Ibid.

[8]Plato, *Crito*, 470.

[9]Skinner, *Beyond Freedom and Dignity*, p. 161.

[10]Skinner, *Science and Human Behavior*, p. 443.

[11]B. F. Skinner, "The Control of Human Behavior," *Transactions of the New York Academy of Sciences*, 17 (May 1955) quoted in Floyd Matson, *The Broken Image* (New York: Anchor/Doubleday, 1966), p. 1.

[12]Skinner's vision is spelled out in an appealing yet frightening fashion in his *Walden Two* (New York: MacMillan, 1948).

Chapter 8: Reinterpreters of the Personal

[1]See Ted Honderich, *Punishment: The Supposed Justifications* (New York: Harcourt, Brace and World, 1970).

[2]See Richard Taylor, *Metaphysics* (Englewood Cliffs: Prentice-Hall, 1963), pp. 54-69.

[3]John Calvin, *The Institutes of the Christian Religion*, trans. Henry Beveridge (Grand Rapids: Eerdmans), II, 206.

[4]Ibid., pp. 206-07.

[5]Ibid., p. 232.

[6]Chapter 5, ii, of the Westminster Confession in *Creeds of the Churches*, rev. ed., ed. John H. Leith (Richmond: John Knox Press, 1973), p. 200.

[7]Ibid., chapter 9, i, p. 205.

[8]See D. M. MacKay, *The Clockwork Image* (Downers Grove: InterVarsity Press, 1974), for an example of a Christian thinker who does not fit either of my categories well. In some respects MacKay takes a Reinterpreter position and in some that of the Limiter of Science. MacKay argues that freedom and determinism must be seen as complementary, not contradictory positions, which sounds like a variation on the Compatibilist position. However he stresses the validity of the concept of agency and argues that from the perspective of the agent at least some acts are rightly viewed as undetermined, which sounds like the view I call Perspectivalism. Perhaps these two positions are not as different as they seem to me. Or perhaps there is some ambivalence in MacKay's thought. I discuss his work in Chapter 9.

Chapter 9: Limiters of Science

[1]See J. C. Eccles, *Brain and Conscious Experience* (New York: Springer-Verlag, 1966) and P. Laslett, ed., *The Physical Basis of Mind* (London: MacMillan, 1950).

[2]See the writings of C. J. Ducasse and C. A. Campbell for a defense of dualism.

[3]See Keith Campbell, *Body and Mind* (Garden City: Anchor/Doubleday, 1970), pp. 41-58 for a review of contemporary criticisms of dualism.

[4]For example, see Malcolm Jeeves, *Psychology and Christianity: The View Both Ways* (Downers Grove: InterVarsity Press, 1976), Chapter 4; J. K. Howard, "The Concept of the Soul in Psychology and Religion," *Journal of The American Scientific Affiliation*, 24, No. 4 (1972), 147-54; Bruce Reichenbach, "Life after Death: Possible or Impossible" and "Re-creation and Personal Identity," *The Christian Scholars Review*, 3, No. 3 (1973), 232-44 and 4, No. 4 (1975), 326-30. Also see Herman Dooyeweerd, *In the Twilight of Western Thought* (Philadelphia: Presbyterian and Reformed Publishing Co., 1960), pp. 157-95.

[5]More on this in Chapter 11.

[6]See Gabriel Marcel, *Creative Fidelity* (New York: Noonday, 1964), particularly the essay "Incarnate Being as the Central Datum of Metaphysical Reflection," for his account of the person.

[7]Maurice Merleau-Ponty, "Prospectus (A Report to the College de France)," reprinted in *Existentialism*, ed. Robert C. Solomon (New York: Random House, 1974), p. 252.

[8]Ibid.

[9]Many of the books in the Studies in Philosophical Psychology Series, ed. R. F. Holland (London: Routledge and Kegan Paul) are good examples. See especially

the works of A. I. Melden, R. S. Peters and Stuart Hampshire.

[10]International Conference on Human Engineering and the Future of Man, Wheaton College, Wheaton, Illinois, July 21, 1975.

[11]MacKay, *The Clockwork Image*, pp. 36-38.

[12]Ibid., pp. 42-44.

[13]Ibid., p. 36.

[14]Gilbert Ryle, *Dilemmas* (London: Cambridge University Press, 1969), pp. 68-81.

[15]Jeeves, p. 18.

[16]Ibid., pp. 33-40; Jeeves's views here closely reflect the work of D. M. MacKay.

[17]MacKay's argument can be found in *Mind*, 69 (1960), 31-40. He has restated the argument in *The Clockwork Image*.

[18]MacKay, *The Clockwork Image*, p. 79.

Chapter 10: Humanizers of Science

[1]A good summary of this view of the hypothetico-deductive method is found in Karl Popper's *The Logic of Scientific Discovery* (New York: Science Editions, 1961), pp. 28-48.

[2]Ibid., pp. 40-42.

[3]R. G. Collingwood, *The Idea of History* (Oxford: Clarendon Press, 1946).

[4]Carl Hempel, "The Function of General Laws in History," reprinted in *Theories of History*, ed. Patrick Gardiner (New York: Free Press of Glencoe, 1959); and Richard Rudner, *The Philosophy of Social Science* (Englewood Cliffs: Prentice-Hall, 1966), pp. 68-83.

[5]Durkheim, rev. of "Essais sur la conception materialiste de l'histoire," pp. 23-24.

[6]Max Weber, *The Theory of Economic and Social Organization* (New York: Oxford University Press, 1947), p. 88.

[7]Ibid., p. 94.

[8]Peter Winch, *The Idea of a Social Science and Its Relation to Philosophy* (New York: Humanities Press, 1958), pp. 124-25.

[9]Ibid., p. 83.

[10]Winch's view here is very close to that which underlies the Generalist's argument.

[11]Abraham Maslow, *Toward a Psychology of Being* (New York: Van Nostrand Reinhold, 1968), p. ix.

[12]See C. Stephen Evans, *Despair: A Moment or a Way of Life?* (Downers Grove: InterVarsity Press, 1972).

[13]T. W. Wann, ed., *Behaviorism and Phenomenology*, paperback edition (Chicago: University of Chicago Press, 1964).

[14]Alfred Schutz, "Concept and Theory Formation in the Social Sciences," in *The Problem of Social Reality*, Collected Papers, ed. Maurice Natanson (The Hague: Martinus Nijhoff, 1962), I, 55-56.

[15]See Alfred Schutz, "The Social World and the Theory of Social Action," in *Studies in Social Theory*, Collected Papers, ed., Arvid Brodersen (The Hague: Martinus Nijhoff, 1964), II, 4.

[16]Stephen Toulmin, *Foresight and Understanding* (Bloomington: Indiana University Press, 1961), p. 27.

[17]Ibid., pp. 27-30.

[18]Ibid., p. 45.

[19]Thomas S. Kuhn, *The Structure of Scientific Revolutions*, 2nd ed. (Chicago:

University of Chicago Press, 1970), p. 111.

[20]N. R. Hanson, *Patterns of Discovery* (London: Cambridge University Press, 1958), pp. 4-30.

[21]This is generally the case with Freudian "unconscious motives," for example, which therefore still preserve a link with the concept of the person as agent.

[22]Bert Hodges has attempted to criticize behaviorism in psychology and argue for a different paradigm in "Toward a Model of Psychological Man and His Science," *The Christian Scholars Review*, 6 (1976), 3-18.

[23]David Lyon, *Christians and Sociology* (Downers Grove: InterVarsity Press, 1975), Chapter 6.

[24]Ibid.

Chapter 11: Recovering the Person: Thinking Christianly about Man

[1]For a detailed consideration of various views of Christianity and culture see H. Richard Niebuhr, *Christ and Culture* (New York: Harper and Row, 1956).

[2]Unless otherwise noted all references to Scripture are taken from the New English Bible.

[3]Of course God's actions do not necessarily have this character.

[4]It is beyond the scope of this essay to give detailed support for this thesis. A careful study of the use of *soul* and *spirit* throughout the Bible is given by Dom Wulstan Mork, *The Biblical Meaning of Man* (Milwaukee: Bruce, 1967).

[5]Some philosophers hold that their weak sense of *identity* is not "identity" at all. Anyone who wishes to restrict the term to its stricter senses can substitute some other term, such as *spatio-temporally coincident*.

[6]Descartes, p. 156.

[7]See Chapter 2, pp. 28-29, for an explanation of contingent identity. I am not certain that this notion of contingent identity is completely coherent; I am merely trying to show that the possibility of life after death seems to remain even on the materialist view, if their claim that the identity of mind and body is contingent is taken at face value.

[8]Jeeves, p. 61.

Chapter 12: Man in a Personal Universe

[1]J. J. C. Smart, "Sensations and Brain Processes," in *The Mind-Brain Identity Theory*, pp. 53-54.

[2]Jean Paul Sartre, *Existentialism and Human Emotions* (New York: Philosophical Library, 1957), p. 15.

[3]Martin Buber, *I and Thou*, trans. Walter Kaufmann (New York: Charles Scribner's Sons, 1970), p. 85.

index

action, nature of, 70-74, 108, 124-28
Adler, Alfred, 128
Allport, Gordon, 128
anomie, 62
Aristotle, 16
Armstrong, D. M., 18
Beck, Lewis White, 76, 160-61
behaviorism, 25-27, 45-57, 105, 119
Berger, Peter, 63, 65n
Berkeley, George, 23
Binswanger, Ludwig, 43-44, 46
Brücke, Ernst, 38
Buber, Martin, 164
Calvin(ism), 95-96, 99
Campbell, C. A., 105n
Campbell, Keith, 25n, 105n
category mistake, 109-10
central-state materialism, 28-29, 49, 104
Collingwood, R. G., 122-23, 127, 128
complementarity, 111-12
computers, 29-32
Comte, Auguste, 16, 17, 60, 88, 119

contingent identity (see identity)
counter-control, 55, 84-85
creation (doctrine of), 140-41, 143, 145-46
cybernetics, 29-32
democracy, 83
Descartes, René, 21, 102-03, 154, 161
Dilthey, Wilhelm, 122
disposition, 27
Dooyeweerd, Herman, 105n
Dreyfuss, Hubert, 30n, 32n
dualism, 22-29, 102-05, 148-49, 153-54
Ducasse, C. J., 105n
Durkheim, Emile, 14-15, 60-62, 124
Eccles, J. C., 104n
empiricism, 16
epiphenomenalism, 24-25, 103
evolution, 9, 24-25
existentialism, 107-08, 128-29, 138
faith and reason, 139-42
Feyerabend, Paul, 132
Freud, Sigmund, 14, 15, 35-44, 56, 64, 128
Fromm, Erich, 128
functionalism, 63-64
Geisteswissenschaften, 122

Goldstein, Kurt, 128
Hampshire, Stewart, 108n, 160-61
Hanson, N. R. 134
Hegel, 23
Hempel, Carl, 123
Hobbes, Thomas, 23
Hodges, Bert, 137n
Holland, R. F., 108n
homo natura, 43, 46
homonculus, 26
Honderich, Ted, 95n
Howard, J. K., 105n
humanist (distinction between senses), 159-60
humanitarian theory of punishment, 11-12
Husserl, Edmund, 130
Huxley, T. H., 25
hypothetico-deductive method, 119-22, 132
ideals of natural order, 133
identity (contingent), 28, 149-50, 150n, 154, 154n
ideology, 64-66
introspection, 47
Jeeves, Malcolm, 105n, 110-11
Kant, 167
Kierkegaard, Soren, 129, 167
Kuhn, Thomas S., 132-35, 142
La Mettrie, 23, 161
law of three stages, 17, 60, 88
Lewis, C. S., 11-12, 54
Lyon, David, 137
machine (definition of), 30
MacKay, Donald M., 31n, 100n, 108-09, 111n, 112-16
Marcel, Gabriel, 107
Marx, Karl, 14, 15, 65, 82-83
Maslow, Abraham, 128-29
materialism, see central-state materialism
May, Rollo, 44n, 129
mechanomorphic hypothesis, 29-32
Melden, A. I., 108n
Merleau-Ponty, Maurice, 107-08
Merton, Robert, 64
methodological behaviorism, 47
Mill, John Stuart, 15
mind-body problem, 21
Mork, Dom Wulstan, 148n
Natureswissenschaften, 122
Niebuhr, H. Richard, 140n
oedipus complex, 39, 41
Orwell, George, 83

paradigms (in science), 134-35, 142
parallelism, 23
Pavlov, 48, 52
Peters, R. S., 108n
phenomenology, 108, 128, 129-31
Plato, 82, 82n
Polanyi, Michael, 32n, 132
Popper, Karl, 120n, 121
positivism (logical), 15-16, 119-20, 132
pragmatic view of science, 111
presuppositions, 43-44
punishment, theories of, 11-13, 95
Putnam, Hilary, 31n
rationalization, 41, 64, 78
redemption, 140-42, 147
Reichenbach, Bruce, 105n
resurrection, 147, 153
retributivist theory of punishment, 11
Rogers, Carl, 128
Rudner, Richard, 123
Ryle, Gilbert, 109-10
Sartre, Jean-Paul, 81, 107, 163-64
Schelling, 23
Schopenhauer, Arthur, 21
Schutz, Alfred, 131
scientism, 18, 88-90, 101-02
Scriven, Michael, 31n
self-stultifying assertion, 76-78
sin, 140-42, 146-47
Skinner, B. F., 14, 15, 17, 25, 45-57, 64, 79, 81-82, 84-85, 135, 156, 160
Smart, J. J. C., 161-62
Smith, C. U. M., 31n
Snow, C. P., 14
sociology of knowledge, 66
Socrates, 82
soul, 22, 102-05, 148-49
spirit, 103, 148
substance, 25
survival after death, 153-54
Szasz, Thomas, 13n
Taylor, Richard, 95n
third-force psychology, 128
Toulmin, Stephen, 132-35, 142
Turing, A. H., 30n
unity of science, 16, 88-90, 119-22
Verstehen, 122-28
Wann, T. W., 130n
Watson, John, 25, 45-48, 51
Weber, Max, 124-25, 127-28, 131
Westminster Confession, 96n, 99
Winch, Peter, 62n, 125-28, 131
Wittgenstein, Ludwig, 108
Woolridge, Dean E., 25n